LISTEN TO LUTHER

DONALD E. DEMARAY

Spiritual Formation Series

Embrace the Spirit	Steven Harper
Cry Joy!	Jerry Mercer
Walk On!	Donald Joy
Celebrate, My Soul!	Reginald Johnson
Listen to Luther	Donald Demaray

Recommended Dewey Decimal Classification: 248.3
Suggested Subject Heading: SPIRITUAL LIFE

Library of Congress Catalog Card Number: 89-60144
ISBN: 0-89693-690-2

VICTOR BOOKS a division of SP Publications, Inc.
Wheaton, Illinois 60187

CONTENTS

FOREWORD

This Spiritual Formation book is for the Christian who hears God's call to a devotional life, and wants to better serve Him in the challenges of every day. It draws on the richness of Christian spirituality through the centuries of church history, but with an application to the twentieth-century believer who is involved in society, rather than withdrawn from it.

Spiritual Formation blends the best of traditional discipleship concepts with the more reflective disciplines of an individual journey toward friendship with God. It is a lifestyle, not a program; a relationship rather than a system; a journey instead of a road map. It calls us into holy partnership with God for our spiritual development.

As you read this book, and then others in the series, I hope that you will receive much more than information. My prayer is that you will experience new levels of formation of your mind and heart, and find yourself drawn closer to Christ.

Steven Harper, General Editor
Associate Professor of Spiritual Formation
Asbury Theological Seminary

PREFACE

Martin Luther's *Table Talk* runs to over 6,500 entries and fills six volumes. No wonder that the work grew to such length! Students and friends recorded the great man's comments with eagerness and frequency.

Luther's wife, Katie, once kiddingly urged her husband to collect tuition for attendance at their table. After all, didn't the students have to pay at the university when he shared his learning and wisdom?

The Luthers' table accommodated quite a circle—their six children, relatives, boarders, and friends. Martin and Katie saw an ever-changing flow of people come and go from their home. This flow helped stimulate the genius and color, the fascination and inspiration, of Luther's comments. In *Table Talk*, he spoke of medicine and miracles, of bright and boring preachers, and made a seemingly endless parade of observations about the simplicities and profundities of human life. His figures of speech added richness to his meanings.

Few communicators match the Reformation founder, sometimes called the Shakespeare of Germany. Yet Luther's oral manner, while sometimes rough, only adds power to his communication.

As you read *Listen to Luther*, drawn and paraphrased from *Table Talk*, be cheered and enriched. Let the fresh winds fill you with the Spirit of Jesus and make you shout with the joyous freedom of the children of God.

Donald E. Demaray
Asbury Theological Seminary
Wilmore, Kentucky
1989

ONE

JESUS CHRIST

1. THE NAME, JESUS CHRIST

All I know about Jesus Christ
    lies in His name.
I have never heard Jesus' actual voice;
I have never seen Jesus' actual body.
    Nonetheless, I am satisfied,
    for I learned about Him from Scripture.
      Praise God!
    I have no need to hear Jesus' voice;
      I have no need to see Jesus in the flesh.
Besides, when everybody rejected me,
    when I was weakest,
      when death made me afraid,
        when wicked, worldly people persecuted me,
    just then I sensed most especially
      the power in the Name,
        Jesus Christ.

This Name often delivered me from death to life.
This Name comforted me in greatest despair,
      especially at the Imperial Assembly,
            Augsburg, 1530, when everyone brushed me aside.
Well! You can be sure, after such rescues,
      that I will live and die for that Name.
I could not yield, even by silence,
      to the false doctrine of Erasmus or anyone else.
I will not tolerate tainting
      the Name of Jesus Christ,
            even with beautiful color or lovely decoration.
I would rather die!
            I would rather suffer plagues
                  and torture with my family!
I would rather come to a shameful end!
I will not smudge the Name, Jesus Christ.

2. THE INDESCRIBABLE MYSTERY

All the world's wisdom
sounds like childish prattle
by comparison to Christ.
      Why?
            Nothing is so wonderful
            as the indescribable mystery
            of the Son of God,
            image of the eternal Father
            who put on human nature.
Jesus helped His earthly father build houses;
Joseph was a carpenter.
            Now, can you picture
            the citizens of Nazareth on Judgment Day,
            when they see Jesus presiding
            in His divine majesty?

They will exclaim to Jesus,
    "You helped build my house!
    How could a carpenter
    be in such a position of honor?"
Jesus cried like all babies,
His mother looked after Him,
as all mothers look after their children.
    He obeyed His parents as He grew up.
    He helped them too.
        Can't you see Him
        taking dinner to His father, Joseph?
He also worried His parents.
    You remember the time he got lost in the crowd?
    Mary must have said when He came back,
        "Dear Jesus,
        where have You been?"
Don't take offense at
the very ordinary life of our Lord.
    Really, there was in Him
    high and divine art and wisdom,
    something very special.
Jesus just humbled Himself,
    even to death on a cross,
        to comfort us—poor, miserable,
            hopeless persons that we are.

3. THE HUMILITY OF CHRIST

The French king
    used to wash a beggar's feet
        on Maundy Thursday.
My! How such humility
    caught the eye and praise of the people.
The Lord of all emperors,

kings, and princes—
the Son of God—
humbled Himself
in the most profound
of all possible ways
when He died on a cross.
But have you noticed
that few wonder at it?
Some do, of course,
the faithful few, His followers.
He abased Himself,
He was despised, plagued, attacked.
And all for us He suffered
this severe embarrassment.

4. THE MEDIATOR

St. Paul tells us that there is only one God,
there is only one Mediator between God and us,
Jesus Christ
who gave Himself
to meet our spiritual needs.
No one of us can get close to God,
no one of us can get grace from God,
except the Mediator help us,
He, you see, is our Advocate.
So, don't do good things to earn God's favor,
and don't expect your honesty, your virtues,
your rewards, your holy living,
your law-abiding style—
don't expect these things
to earn you forgiveness of sins.
Not even the saints earn their justification.
Stop to think how angry God is at sin.

We have all sinned.
But good news!
Jesus became the go-between
so you and I can know
the joy of forgiveness.

5. CONVERSATION AT THE LAST SUPPER

The conversation at the Last Supper
between Christ and His disciples
was beautiful, loving, and friendly.
Jesus talked to them
with the love of a father
for his children.
He listened to them,
knowing their weaknesses
and their naive attitudes.
Philip said, "Show us the Father."
Thomas said, "We don't know the way."
Peter said, "I will go to death with You."
Each one freely expressed himself.
Do you see the beauty in that conversation?
Jesus listened with full acceptance,
never rejecting the disciples.

6. CHRIST'S MISSION

Money? Wealth? Earthly kingdom?
Christ had none of these,
yet He gave what He had
to kings and princes.
But observe His real mission:
He conquered sin, death,
the devil, and hell.

He saves all who believe Him,
through His Word.

7. THE SUFFERINGS OF CHRIST

Ponder the sufferings in the garden,
    the sweat and blood,
    the other noble spiritual sufferings
        no human being can either know or imagine.
    If we should even begin
    to feel those sufferings,
        we would die right away.
Many people die of grief,
for the heart's sorrow can be death itself.
    But if we should feel such anguish
    and pain as Christ experienced,
        the soul could not remain
        in the body to endure it.
Body and soul would split apart.
        Only Christ could cope,
            and He produced bloody sweat.

8. FAITH VERSUS WORKS

Nothing is more sure than this:
    refusal to take hold of Christ by faith
    robs us of comfort;
        more, Christ becomes a curse,
        and He remains a curse
        until faith takes hold.
Here's the law at work:
    The more we labor to get grace,
    the less we know how to take hold of Christ.

Indeed, the more He is unknown by faith,
the more we cannot expect counsel, help, or comfort,
even though we die in the attempt.

9. CHRIST BECAME SIN FOR US

All the prophets saw by the Spirit
that Christ would become
sin and sacrifice
for the whole world.
He was forsaken;
He took the burden of all sin:
St. Paul's sins—
he blasphemed God
and persecuted the church;
St. Peter's sins—
he denied Christ;
David's sins—
he was an adulterer and murderer,
and brought disgrace to the Lord
as the pagans looked on.
Moses' law judged sinners.
Jesus' enemies saw Him breaking the law
though He was innocent.
Outright sinners and "sophisticated" people
obscured the picture of Jesus
taking the world's sin and guilt
and delivering from the curse of the law.
Sophisticated people today want us only
to follow Christ's example,
But this robs Christ of His purpose
and leaves God an angry judge.

10. THE TRIUMPHAL ENTRY

Our blessed Saviour rode into Jerusalem
    in very poor circumstances;
the King of heaven and earth
    sat on a donkey covered
    with His disciples' clothes.
    This powerful Potentate
    looked poverty-stricken!
Zechariah prophesied all this,
and Scripture came to fulfillment.
    Jesus came into Jerusalem in stately glory
        and something about the prophesies
    brings that heavenly dignity to focus.
        The world sees His entry as poor,
    with a kind of bargain-basement feel to the episode.
Christ did not mention this prophecy,
but the apostles and evangelists used it as a witness.
    Christ, on the other hand, preached and wept,
    and the people showed their respect
        by olive branches and palms,
        signs of peace and victory.

11. WHO CRUCIFIED CHRIST?

Jews crucified Christ with words,
but Gentiles crucified Him with works and acts.
Actually, His sufferings prophesied our wickedness;
    indeed, Christ suffers to this day,
        even more in the Church
            than in the synagogue,
    and with greater blasphemy,
        contempt,
            and iron-handedness.

Let me document. In some places,
when faith and Judgment Day come to focus,
    leaders say, "Oh! Do you believe that?
    Take on happy, merry ways
        to cover your feelings.
    Don't let your mind
        even think about faith and judgment."
These kinds of blasphemies, common today,
leave people without fear of punishment,
and enhance the communication of false beliefs.

12. THE SECOND COMING OF CHRIST

The prophets preached Christ's Second Coming,
        as we do now.
    We know the Last Day will arrive,
    but we do not know what
    the next life will be like.
On the other hand, we have general ideas.
True Christians will live in everlasting joy,
        peace, and wholeness.
The prophets said He would come soon.
They gave a name to the day of the Messiah,
        the Last Day;
the prophets said the signs
    of the first and second comings were the same,
        almost as if they would happen at one time.
In Corinthians Paul spoke to those
who wondered if Christ would come in their day.
    Christ Himself talked about signs
    and how they would appear.
        How I would love to be on earth
        with Christ our Saviour
            when He comes in joy!

13. HE DESCENDED INTO HELL

Christ descended into hell. Why?
    To put the devil in chains;
    to bring him to judgment.
People who like to argue say that
    Infernus (hell) means grave.
I have problems with that because:
    The Hebrew *Nabot* means pit,
    and *Scola* or *Gehenna* (hell) is added.
The ancients made four different hells.

14. THE FELLOWSHIP OF CHRIST

What was the nature of the communion or fellowship
of our blessed Saviour, Jesus Christ?
Doubtless loving and family-like.
    Equal with God, yet a person like us;
        He committed no sin,
    yet He saw Himself suffering no dishonor;
        but He was service-oriented—
    He waited on His disciples at table,
        as my servant waits on me;
    yet He accepted the disciples
        who took His serving for granted.
So the bottom line is this:
    "He came to minister,
    not to be ministered to."
        He is high example!
        He humbled Himself and suffered,
    yet He created the world,
        heaven and earth and all in them;
    with a single finger
        He could have upset His creation.

15. CHRIST, SURE RULER OF HIS KINGDOM

Wonderful, the way Christ rules His kingdom!
  He conceals Himself,
     so His presence goes unseen;
yet He puts emperors to shame, and kings too,
  and all else who think they're pretty good—
    all who see themselves as wise,
      powerful, and superior judges.
  But in Him belongs a *Plerophoria,*
    a complete assurance,
  that He is *the* Ruler of the kingdom
    to which we belong.
Now more about our Ruler:
  He is the beginning and end
  of all my thought about religion,
  daytime thoughts, and nighttime too.
He is so big that I have only inklings
  of the height, depth, and breadth
of this incomprehensible and endless wisdom;
  I have only fragments
    of this deep and precious wisdom.

16. CHRIST'S WORK

Yes, Christ explains the law;
  yes, Christ does miracles;
    but these cannot compare
      with His chief work.
  The prophets
  and especially the apostles
  did miracles too.
Christ's special work is this:

to combat the law, sin, and death
    for the whole world.
to take on Himself the law,
    our sin, also our death,
to come through all that with victory,
    overcoming and destroying them,
        thus releasing the desolate
        from sin and evil.

17. CHRIST COMFORTS THE DESPAIRING

Christ the Saviour has come.
But He does not help hypocrites,
    nor the proud,
    nor those who don't respect God,
    nor people who condemn others,
    nor rascals.
You see, all these think there is no grace,
        refuse to expect comfort,
        and say the law is something to fear.
Who, then, does Christ help?
    Those who sometimes feel the law threatens them.
    Those who do not give way to despair in trial.
    Those who, with proper confidence, go to Him.
        In His presence they meet grace,
        just there He delivers them.

18. AFRAID OF CHRIST?

Such a shame—that we always fear Christ!
    But why?
Never in heaven or earth a more loving man,
        a more family kind of person,
        a more nonthreatening man.

And these characteristics express themselves in
>His words,
>His works,
>His style.
More, He related with empathy to the
>poor,
>sorrowful,
>and to those with tormented consciences.
Now is it any wonder to you
>that the prophet Jeremiah prays,
>>"O Lord, help us not to be afraid of You"?

19. THE WISDOM OF THE LORD

Psalm 51 touches the mystery:
>"Behold! You require truth
>inside us,
>and You make me
>understand wisdom secretly."
This is the mystery hidden from the world,
and it will stay hidden.
>This is the truth inside us,
>>the secret wisdom.
Note that this is not the wisdom of
>lawyers,
>physicians,
>philosophers,
>crafty people of the world.
To the contrary,
>This is the wisdom of the Lord:
>>You make me understand it;
>this is the Golden Art;
>this is what Sadoleto didn't have,
>>even though he wrote about Psalm 51.

20. *CHRIST TAKES CARE OF HIS OWN*

The devil assaults Christians,
With high power and subtlety,
   he vexes true Christians through
      tyrants,
      heretics,
      "Christians" who are not real,
      and an aggressively opposing world.
By contrast Christ resists
the devil and his kingdom through
      a few uncomplicated people,
      some unjustly smeared,
      people the world sees
         as weak and foolish.
But note this:
      Christ comes out on top!
What an unequal war if one lonely sheep
had to encounter 100 wolves!
      Christ sent the apostles into the world,
         one after another suffered martyrdom.
Against wolves you would think
      we would send lions,
         or even more ferocious beasts.
But that's not Christ's way:
      He translates our weakness and foolishness
         into wisdom and power.
He allows those who oppose
      His servants and disciples
         to harvest exactly what they sow.
The bottom line:
      He alone, Lord of Hosts,
         does great things.
      He takes care of His sheep among wolves.

He lets us see that God's power,
    not human wisdom,
    does the job.
Even if He would allow one sheep eaten by wolves,
    He would send two or more
        to take the place of that sheep.

21. THOSE WEAK IN FAITH

Those weak in faith also belong to Christ's kingdom.
    Otherwise Christ would not have said to Peter,
        "Strengthen your friends."
    Otherwise Paul would not have said,
        "Receive the weak in faith."
    Otherwise Paul would not have encouraged us,
        "Comfort the feebleminded and
            support the weak."
If the weak in faith didn't belong to Christ,
    what would have become of the apostles?
    Notice that the Lord had to deal with them
        even after His resurrection,
            even to reproving them for unbelief.

22. CHRIST THE PHYSICIAN

Thirsty?
    A cup of cold water quenches thirst,
    if one can have nothing better.
Hungry?
    A morsel of bread stills hunger,
    if one is really hungry.
Ill?
    People will travel 100 miles
    for medical assistance.

Christ is the best, the surest,
the only medicine against
the most fearful enemy, the devil.
But only the few and the weak stick to Christ,
the true Physician.
By His art they learn what
holy Simeon knew well when he sang,
"Lord, now let Your servant go in peace,
for I have seen Your salvation!"
Where did Simeon get his great joy?
He saw the world's Saviour,
the true Physician against sin and death.
How painful to see
a thirsty person go for water,
even just a cup!
How painful to see
a hungry person go for bread,
even just a morsel.
Thirsty and hungry people can go
only two or three hours without help.
Spiritually hungry and thirsty people seem to go
a long time before they really desire
the best of physicians:
This in spite of the fact that
He lovingly calls us to Himself:
"You who are thirsty,
come to Me and drink."

23. HIDDEN IN CHRIST

Just as Christ is invisible and unknown to the world,
So Christians are invisible and unknown to the world.
"Your life," says St. Paul,
"is hid with Christ in God."

So the world doesn't know us,
and the world doesn't see Christ in us.
We separate ourselves from the world:
We are crucified to the world,
the world is crucified to us.
In other words,
The world cares nothing for us,
we care nothing for the world.
Let the world go with its wealth,
we stick to our mind and manners.
To have Christ, in love,
is to be rich and happy enough!
We care nothing for the state of the world,
nor for its honor or its wealth.
But often we lose our Saviour
and forget He lives in us
and that we live in Him.
We forget He belongs to us
and that we belong to Him.
Though He seems hidden from us in a time of need,
we find comfort in His promise,
"I am with you daily
to the end of the world."
Now that's the richest treasure!

24. *THE IMMEASURABLE GOODNESS OF CHRIST*

I expect more goodness from my wife, Kate,
from my friends, from Philip Melanchthon,
than from my dear Saviour, Christ Jesus.
Yet I am very sure neither Kate nor any friend,
can possibly suffer for me as Christ suffered for me.
Why, then, should I be afraid of Him?

My foolish weakness grieves me!
Plainly, the Gospels show Him
    mild and gentle toward His disciples;
        He passed over their weaknesses
        with kindness;
            He overlooked their presumption
            and foolishness;
            He dealt with their unbelief in tenderness.
The Scripture promises that He blesses
all who put their trust in Him.
    So stop your unbelief, stop your fear.
    He is more loving, friendly,
    considerate and compassionate towards us than
            our relatives,
            our brothers and sisters in the Church,
            parents to their children.
So when you have temptations,
assure yourself that Christ doesn't bring them!
    They are brought by the envious devil
    who frightens and wounds us,
    and would like to destroy Christ,
        for Christ comforts, heals, revives.
        Such grace and goodness!
        How immeasurable!
    But we can understand it
        only under great trial.
Case study:
Tyrants and untrue Christians
    attacked me fiercely.
        Without that attack
    I would have thought too highly of myself
    and focused on my own dexterity and expertise.
        Without that attack
    I would not have prayed so hard for help.

Without that attack
I would have taken the credit,
I would have overlooked God's grace, source of all!
You can see how the devil almost got me.
But to prevent this, Christ
allowed my torment, inwardly and outwardly.
"It is good for me
that I've been in trouble,
so I could learn God's laws."

25. CHRIST VERSUS THE DEVIL

Little wonder that Satan opposes
Christ, His people, His kingdom.
Little wonder he sets himself
against all that is good
with intense cunning and power.
His hate is old, it began in Paradise.
By nature, good and evil possess
contrary minds and dispositions.
The devil smells Christ 100 miles away;
he hears when people preach against his kingdom,
when they preach in Constantinople,
Rome, or Wittenberg.
He feels his hurts and damage,
and only rages and enhances his battle
with greater horror.
But we must wonder even more
at the battle within Christ's kingdom,
the battle through the bond of love.
Instead of love, we have
envy, hate,
bitterness, disharmony,
and even readiness to kill!

A man and his wife can be very close,
and a father and a son too;
    mothers and daughters,
    sisters and brothers,
    can love one another very much.
        Yet, incompatibility
    and hard feelings creep in.

26. CHRIST AND LAW

Impossible! That law and gospel
could live in one heart.
It's this simple:
    You can't have it both ways—
        either it's Christ
        or it's law.
St. Paul put it this way:
    "Those who think they are
    justified through the Law
    have fallen from grace."
When you get in the frame of mind
    that says Christ and the law
    can live in the same house,
        forget it!
            The devil's made a hit.
To put it another way,
    the devil's masked a lie
        to look like Christ.
That awareness will paralyze you with fear!
Christ never calls on you to trust your good works;
    Christ does say, "Come to Me
        when you're fatigued and discouraged,
        and I will rest you."

27. LOOK AT CHRIST THREE WAYS

We should look at accounts of Christ
three ways:
    As history—
        the stories of His acts.
    As a gift.
    As example—
        Christ is our Role Model
        for belief and living.

✝ JESUS CHRIST

Since, then, you have been raised with Christ, set your hearts on things above, where Christ is seated at the right hand of God. Set your minds on things above, not on earthly things. For you died, and your life is now hidden with Christ in God.

Colossians 3:1-3

HIS PRESENCE

Ask God for Himself.
His presence is preeminent.

GOD'S WORD

In your own words, summarize the verses above.
Can you think of similar Scriptures?
What is the heart of this passage?
Do you know someone who lives this way?

SELF-EXAMINATION

What is the good news for you in these verses?
What sin, now uncovered, must you confess?
What will you do to put hands and feet to your faith?

PETITION

Pray for yourself, in light of God's message.

INTERCESSION

Now you are ready to pray for others.

TWO

GOD'S WORD

1. THE BIBLE

The Scriptures are like a fruit orchard.
    All kinds of trees grow there.
    All sorts of fruit àre harvested.
The Bible, rich in variety, offers us
    priceless comfort,
    wisdom,
    counsel,
    cautions,
    assurances,
    warnings against dangers.
I have shaken every tree in this orchard,
        and got at least a couple
        of apples or pears
            from each one.

2. HOW I KNOW THE BIBLE IS GOD'S WORD

My proofs go like this:
    Just as the world was and is,
        so Moses wrote in his first book.
    Even as God made the world,
        so it was, is, and remains.
    Alexander the Great,
    Egypt, Babel, Persia, Greece,
    the Roman rulers Julius and Augustus—
        all these worked fiercely
           to suppress *and* destroy the Bible,
           yet they all found their hands tied.
They—rulers, nations, empires—
    are gone! Vanished!
        But the Bible stays on and on,
        stays the same . . . just as it was written.
Who preserves the Bible
    against its would-be destroyers?
Who defends it?
    No man or woman; only God Himself,
        the Lord of the Scriptures.
           What a wonder!
The Bible has been preserved,
    though the devil and the world
        are its enemies.
The devil has destroyed many good books;
    he has done away with many saints
        (some we don't know about).
    He only pretends to leave the Bible alone.
Similarly, baptism, the Lord's Supper,
    and preaching have all stayed with us
    in spite of those who opposed them.
        God keeps and maintains them.

Homer, Virgil, and ancient writers
   of equal note are profitable,
      but in comparison to the Bible,
      they are nothing.

3. THE DIFFERENCE BETWEEN THE BIBLE AND OTHER BOOKS

Well, for starters—
   grace and truth.
Pagan books?
   Faith, hope and love just aren't there.
   Those books limit themselves to this world:
      what human beings can see,
      what ordinary insight comprehends,
   but nothing of hope in the Lord.
Take just two books—Psalms and Job.
   In that pair we see
      faith and hope,
      patience and prayer.
The short and long of it is this:
   The Holy Scripture is
      the best Book of God,
      the supreme Book of God.
   It is full of comfort
      in crisis and temptations.
Why?
   It communicates faith, hope, and love,
   and that way beyond our ability
      to work through in our heads.
In fact, the Scriptures tell us how
      faith, hope, and love
   throw light on our anxieties and frustrations.
The Bible also tells us

that after this life
with all its difficulties
    we can live in heaven eternally.

4. OUR CHIEF AIM IN GETTING INTO THE BIBLE

Our chief aim: *Truly to know Christ.*
    You will find Him friendly,
    you will find Him familiar,
        like pictures in a family photo album.
No wonder St. Peter asked us
        "to grow in knowledge of Christ."
Christ Himself told us
    that we learn about Him
    only in the Scriptures:
        "Look diligently in the Scriptures:
        They testify about Me."
One thing we must not do:
    critique Scripture—
        as if we had ability to do that!
But we must do this:
    diligently,
    prayerfully,
    searchingly
        meditate on Scripture.
    Evil wants us to critique Scripture
    through the spectacles of our own reason.
In fact, God uses our trials and temptations
    to interpret Scripture to us.
Diligent and rational study
    just won't give us
        realistic scriptural insight.
The Holy Spirit is our Teacher.

Youth and learning must submit
        to this Teacher.
When temptation attacks me,
        I grab hold of a passage
                and fix my grip on it.
Jesus Himself gives me the passage that says,
        "CHRIST DIED FOR ME."
                That's comforting!
So I as a pastor counsel:
Draw water from the pure spring—
        STUDY THE BIBLE.
        You are a true scholar
        if you ground yourself
        in Scripture.
One text from the Bible surpasses
many other writings which lack
        strength,
        soundness, and
        documentation.
        Take, for example, Paul's text,
        "Everything is good
        if accepted with thanks."
This text tells us that
What God made is good.
        So eating, drinking, marriage
        are God's making
                and therefore good.
But some commentators
        "misread" this text,
        really canceling it out.
Not me! I take the text
        over the commentators.

5. BUILD YOUR FOUNDATION ON SCRIPTURE

Want to build a really good foundation?
    Then ground yourself in the Bible.
        Scripture gives you sure footing and
        makes it hard to run blithely on in error.
This applies most assuredly to preachers too.
    I myself have conquered false teachers with Scripture.
        I have even surprised and astonished them.
        I have also found them lazy.
    They interpret Scripture with reason alone.
    They don't take Holy Scripture seriously.
        They are like the Pharisees
        who heard Jesus say,
            "Do this and live,"
        but didn't follow through.
Secular man and seducing spirits
    just don't understand Scripture,
    but with self-excusing writings
        run into error.
But one armed with Scripture holds the truth.
    To take the commentators as authority,
        instead of the Bible,
    issues in terrible wrongs.

6. THE BIBLE HEADS THE ARTS

Don't lose the Bible!
    With all diligence and in the fear of God,
        PREACH THE BIBLE.
If the Bible taught stands supreme,
    we're home free.
The Bible is the Head Dean,

Dean of all faculties,
    Dean of all arts.
But if theological studies fall and fail,
    count on it—
        what's left has no value!

7. ENEMIES AND LOVERS OF GOD'S WORD

People who hate God's Word
    signal both consolation and warning.
Consolation:
    Thank God for the blessing of
        loving God's Word,
        hearing it seriously,
        learning from it,
        delighting in it.
Warning:
    To hate God, His Word, and the ministers of it
    means punishment and severe judgment.
        This is what happens to those
        unwilling to hear the Word.

8. BIBLE TRANSLATION: TWO RULES

First: Is a passage unclear?
    Ask: Does the material deal with
        grace or law,
        forgiveness or wrath?
    This question often leads to clarity
        for the most perplexing excerpt,
        because God divides truth into
        law and gospel.
    This law-and-gospel principle
        reduces all things to the bottom line.

In theology we have just law and gospel,
    One or the other.
    So every prophet either
        threatens or teaches,
        terrifies and judges or promises.
    Everything comes to this either/or.
Second: Is the meaning ambiguous?
    I ask people with a better knowledge of language,
        "Does the Hebrew really say
            what I think it says?
        Does my suggested translation mesh
            with the overall message of the book?"
Some lose their way because they do not know
    the actual contents of Bible books.
    But to know true substance
        is to have a handle on better translation.

9. SCRIPTURE TRUTH: WE LEARN IT BY PATIENCE AND PRACTICE

"Sophisticated" people see
    the rejection of the church and
    the glorification of the world.
This evaluation comes from
    Reason without God's Word.
"Sophisticates" hate all religion.
    They say the Resurrection is an invention
        to frighten plain people.
Peasants, on the other hand,
    don't hate God and religion;
        They scarcely think of "sophisticated" things.
But "clever" people find interest in these things,
    ponder them,
    evaluate them by reason.

Erasmus is an example.
Another is the Epicureans.
We, however, know the confirmation of Scripture,
 by miracles like the raising of the dead
 and the casting out of demons.
No wonder the Lord God tells us so often
 to live by the Holy Bible.
Now I didn't learn Scripture truth all at once.
 I thought long and hard about it;
 I went through spiritual testing;
  I'm glad about those trials
  because learning comes with practice.
Fanatics and tainted sectarians don't grasp this.
No one masters an art without practice.
 Would you like to have a doctor
 who only reads books?
 No, for he learns more and more
  by working with patients,
  by watching nature heal.
   He knows, then, that
   he has lots more to learn!
Why not learn Scripture
  by experience too? . . .
  learn by knocking heads
  with the opposition.
 But what a fulfillment
 when at last I can say,
  Eureka! I've found the ring of truth.
Some think sermon listening is enough to teach them.
 Zwingli erred,
 supposing he knew it all,
 and supposing Scripture truth to be easy.
True, Scripture is enough,
 but I must find *right* texts.

When I'm tempted to believe
    that God does not treat me graciously,
    I'd better not quote 1 Corinthians 2:9,
       "No eye has seen,
       nor ear heard,
       nor the heart of man conceived,
       what God has prepared
       for those who love Him."
Not that text, for the tempter will say,
  "You have not loved God!"
Nor can I deny that simply because
    I'm a serious Scripture reader or a preacher.
      My feet don't fit those shoes!
But I can say,
      "Jesus died for me!
      God forgives my sins!"
        Now *there's* winning truth.

10. HERETICS PROVOKE US TO SEARCH THE SCRIPTURES

You wish to be a theologian?
    Master the Scriptures.
    Master them so you can answer
      anyone who attacks a passage.
    Another way of putting this:
      Learn to distinguish law and gospel.
If I could do that perfectly, I would never be sad.
    Whoever understands
    the law-and-gospel principle of interpretation
      is a winner.
All Scripture is either law or gospel.
      The law leads to despair;
      the gospel leads to salvation.

I learn more about this daily,
for the gospel spells LIFE.
The Pope drove me to this principle;
he opened my eyes.
    St. Augustine observed that heretics
        provoke us to search Scripture;
Otherwise we wouldn't bother.

11. I READ THE BIBLE THROUGH TWICE A YEAR

I read the Bible through
two times a year.
    The Bible is like
a grand and immense tree.
        Every word is a small branch.
        I shake every branch,
            wanting to know its meaning.

12. LIGHT TO UNDERSTAND THE BIBLE

A great light
shines on Scripture
so that we can understand it.
    The scholars who used just their heads
    couldn't explain the Scriptures to us.
        Augustine was an exception,
            but others suffered blindness.
            Read Scripture first;
                afterward study Augustine;
            He was a sharp analyst.
My best advice:
    Go to the Source and
    diligently study it.

To know the text is
to be an exceptional theologian.
        To know one passage well is
        to be ahead of four
        unreliable commentators.
Take, for example, this text:
        "Everything created by God is good."
Well, commentators like
Bernard, Dominic, and Basil
        thought differently and
        lived contrary to that text.
Now note:
        The text itself proves its own truth,
        contradicting these commentators. . . .
The Holy Spirit won't be in jail
to the mere words of commentators.
        What He will do is this:
        Reveal true meanings.
I once got stuck on words
        and missed true meanings.
Some scholars got me focusing so hard
on Greek words—definitions and all that—
        that I couldn't see
        the practical meanings.

13. SEE SCRIPTURE WITH YOUR OWN EYES

Will you look at the flood of books!
        Everybody wants to write a book
        to feed his own pride.
                Some write a book
                for personal gain.
But in the welter of volumes about the Bible
        we can lose the Bible!

A good way to neglect the text!
(Even though the writers may be the best.)
As a young person
    I mastered the Bible.
    Reading and rereading
    made me familiar with it,
        like a well-used footpath.
Well, I didn't consult the scholars
    until after mastery.
        But finally I put them aside
        so I could do my own work,
            my own observing and wrestling.
Here's the principle:
    See with your own eyes—
        that's better than
            seeing with another's.
Now you understand why I wish
I could bury all my books.
    I don't want people imitating me,
        and certainly not trying
        to get famous writing books,
            as if Christ died for their glory
            instead of the honor of His Name!

14. HUMBLE STUDY

Assume the humble posture toward the Bible that says,
    "Teach me! Teach me! Teach me!"
God's Spirit resists proud students.
    Even diligent students.
        Even those who once preached
            Christ from pure motives.
        God excludes the proud from the Church.
Proud people have a way of turning into heretics.

Warning: Gifted people quickly become arrogant.
    God does adorn some with great gifts;
    He also ducks them in the cold waters of trial
    to teach them they're nothing.
        So Paul had a thorn in the flesh
        to keep him from pride.
        So, too, Philip Melanchthon had
        problems to keep him from strange ideas.
    But some gifted people are haughty and
    thumb their noses at teachers and learning.
        I fear these people have had it!
Pride drove the angel from heaven;
    pride ruins lots of preachers.
        Study sacred things with a humble spirit.

15. THE PLAIN MEANING OF SCRIPTURE

I was such a smart young man,
Especially before I studied theology!
    In those days I handled
        teachings ("allegories"),
        morals ("tropologies"),
        the future ("analogies")
            in such a "learned" way.
I knew all the tricks of the trade.
        Today, if I were to use them,
        they'd be looked upon as antiques;
        I now know they are garbage.
So you can see why I've stopped using
these tricks of interpretation.
    Today I just look for
    the plain meanings in Scripture.
        Why?

In the obvious sense of the Bible I find
  renewal, comfort,
      energy, adequacy,
          genuine learning.
And why not the tricks?
    They may make a big impression,
        but they are really monkey business.

GOD'S WORD

All Scripture is God-breathed and is useful for teaching, rebuking, correcting and training in righteousness, so that the man of God may be thoroughly equipped for every good work.

2 Timothy 3:16-17

HIS PRESENCE

Ask God for Himself.
His presence is preeminent.

GOD'S WORD

In your own words, summarize the verses above.
Can you think of similar Scriptures?
What is the heart of this passage?
Do you know someone who lives by these verses?

SELF-EXAMINATION

What is the good news for you in these verses?
What sin, now uncovered, must you confess?
What will you do to put hands and feet to your faith?

PETITION

Pray for yourself, in light of God's message.

INTERCESSION

Now you are ready to pray for others.

THREE

THE HOLY SPIRIT

1. WHAT THE HOLY SPIRIT DOES

The Holy Spirit holds two offices:
    Grace—
        that means God favors us,
        and accepts us as His
        for Christ's sake.
    Prayer—
        He prays for us and the world,
        asking all evil to turn away
        and all good to come to us.
    The Spirit of grace teaches;
    the Spirit of prayer prays.
It's one thing to look forward to the Holy Spirit,
    even to have Him as many did before Christ;
        yet it is quite another thing
        to be aware of Him by revelation.
The Holy Spirit Himself is the certainty;

that makes us sure of the Word.
        And note, too, that the Holy Spirit
        comes to no one without the Word.
Non-Christians have no certainty;
they cannot be sure of the things of God,
        for they depend not on the Word
        but on their own goodness.
        Even after many great works they doubt:
        "Who knows if our acts please God?
        Who knows if we have done enough?"
They must think to themselves,
        "We are not worthy even now."
                But true Christians
                put such doubts behind them.
They focus
        neither on their holiness
        nor on their unworthiness.
        They trust Jesus Christ
            who is holy and worthy.
                Jesus *is* the Christian's
                holiness and worthiness.
Well now, I am a poor sinner;
the Bible makes that clear.
        Only the Holy Spirit can say,
        "Christ is Lord."
        Only the Holy Spirit teaches,
            preaches, and declares Christ.
The Holy Spirit
        paves the way for teaching;
the Holy Spirit
        applies the heard Word.
So we hear the Word,
        then the Spirit works it into us;
                He works in whom He wills,

how He wills,
and never without the Word.

2. WHITSUNDAY

The Holy Spirit began His work openly
        on Pentecost Day, what we call Whitsunday.
He gave the apostles genuine comfort;
He gave them secure and joy-filled courage.
        They didn't care what the world said,
        nor did they care what the devil said,
        nor yet whether friends and enemies
        responded with anger or pleasure.
                With security they took to city streets
                with thoughts like these:
                        "Never mind Annas, Caiaphas,
                        Pilate, or Herod;
                        they don't rule us;
                        we rule them!"
The loving apostles did the work
        with all courage,
        never seeking escape,
        never taking unfair advantage of people.
They never asked if they should preach;
        they just went boldly on;
        they opened their mouths freely;
        they reproved people—
                rulers and subjects—
                all as murderers,
                wicked wretches, and traitors
                who killed life's Author.
And what about us today?
        The Spirit was a must for the apostles;
        the Spirit is a must for us.

Adversaries give us a bad time,
            as they did the apostles,
        as disturbers of the peace
            do against the Church.
When something goes wrong,
        these adversaries say
            that we Christians are to blame!
        That since the Reformation,
            evil is on a rampage.
        That since the Reformation,
            we have had famine, wars, enemies.
        That all these things have come
            since Protestant preaching.
These adversaries would like to say that
        we caused the devil's fall from heaven
            and that we crucified Christ.
Now can you see why Whitsuntide sermons
on the Holy Spirit are a must?
        We need comfort.
        We need boldness
            to condemn blasphemy.
        We need courage
            to move forward
            despite offenders,
            reproachers, heretics.
        We need courage
            that cares for nothing,
            preaches Christ,
            acknowledges the crucified Jesus.
The preached gospel offends people the world over;
It suffers rejection and a terrible dressing-down.
        If the gospel did not offend,
        if it were fine and agreeable,
        people would love hearing it.

But because the gospel angers especially
    the famous,
    the powerful,
    the sophisticated,
a whole lot of courage
from the Holy Spirit
    is necessary for true preachers.
Note the courage of the apostles,
poor fishermen that they were.
    They had to stand on their hind legs and
preach to the whole Jerusalem council,
    which was very upset.
        The government threatened the apostles;
        the spiritual leaders threatened them;
        the Roman emperor threatened them.
So you see why their preaching
had to be supported by the Holy Spirit.
    Wonder of wonders
        that the high priest didn't kill them,
        that Pontius Pilate didn't kill them.
You see, their preaching smacked of rebellion
    against the religious authorities,
    against the governmental authorities.
But look what happened:
    The high priest and Pilate
    were gripped by fear.
    God demonstrated His power
    through weak apostles.
And so it is with the Church of Christ:
    It moves ahead in apparent weakness,
        yet in mighty strength,
    so Mr. Worldly Wiseman will look
        in amazement and fear.

3. TRUE AND CONSTANT COMFORTER

Both Scripture and the Nicene Creed teach that
>   the Holy Spirit brings life
>   and calls for worship,
>   along with Father and Son.
>>   The Holy Spirit,
>>   true and enduring
>>   with Father and Son,
>>   is one with God.
You can see that if He were not
>   true and everlasting God,
He could not have divine power,
>   not honor, nor life,
>   nor yet worship,
>   nor glory either.
>>   Read the Fathers of the Church:
>>   they held firmly to this belief.
The comfort of the Holy Spirit
differs from the world's comfort,
>   for in the world
>>   we do not have authentic faithfulness.
>   But the Holy Spirit
>   never deceives,
>   never lies.
We call the Spirit a witness
>   because He testifies for Christ
>>   and for Christ only.
>>>   Without this witness
>>>   we would have no comfort.
True and firm comfort rest on Christ.
That's why we take sure hold of Christ and say,
>   "I believe in Jesus;
>   He died for me."

The Holy Spirit preaches only Christ;
that preaching comforts all sad hearts.
      Just here I stand,
   leaning on no other source of comfort.
Jesus Himself says the Holy Spirit
   is everlasting and the all-powerful God.
That is the basis of His commission:
   "Go teach all nations;
   baptize them in the name of
      the Father,
      the Son,
      the Holy Spirit;
   teach them to live after My pattern
   in all things."
Jesus also says,
   "I pray to the Father
   to give you another Comforter,
   One who will live with you always;
   this Comforter is the Spirit of Truth,
      and the world cannot receive Him,
      because the world cannot see Him.
         The world just can't understand Him."
Underscore that sentence about Jesus
praying to His Father to send you another Comforter.
   Note the persons:
      the Father,
      the Son.
   The Son prays;
   the Father hears;
      yet neither is the Comforter.
      The Scripture plainly
      pictures three Persons;
      Yet the three are One.
Jesus clarifies the whole teaching:

"When the Comforter comes,
the One I will send from the Father,
the Spirit of truth,
who comes from the Father,
He will make clear who I am."
    Notice that Jesus indicates
    the work of the Holy Spirit,
    also the essence of the Spirit.
    He has no beginning and
    He is everlasting.
        No wonder the prophets call Him
        "the Spirit of the Lord."

THE HOLY SPIRIT

If you love Me, you will obey what I command. And I will ask the Father, and He will give you another Counselor to be with you forever—the Spirit of truth. The world cannot accept Him, because it neither sees Him nor knows Him. But you know Him, for He lives with you and will be in you.

John 14:15-17

HIS PRESENCE

Ask God for Himself.
His presence is preeminent.

GOD'S WORD

In your own words, summarize the verses above.
What is the heart of this passage?
Do you know someone who has made the Holy Spirit his Counselor?

SELF-EXAMINATION

What is the good news for you in these verses?
What sin, now uncovered, must you confess?
What will you do to put hands and feet to your faith?

PETITION

Pray for yourself, in light of God's message.

INTERCESSION

Now you are ready to pray for others.

FOUR

PRAYER

1. PRAYER AND GOD'S PROMISE

When we pray
    we have this promise—
        what we ask, we get, but not
           in our wished-for shape.
Without the James 5:16 promise,
I would not bother praying.
    But God knows what He's doing
    when He shapes answers
        His way rather than our way.
           Otherwise we'd want everything on our terms!
God acts the same in both life and death matters.
That I know from frequent experience.
If we pray with genuine earnestness,
    He will hear,
        even though answers surprise us
          in their shape and timing.

Otherwise faith would be worthless.
So prayer is hard going.
I know very well what praying involves.
No, I haven't committed adultery,
but I have broken the first three
commandments against God and His Word.
My big sins against these commandments
keep me from facing my sins
against the next set of commandments.

2. STRICT PRAYERS

While a monk,
I refused to miss
the stated prayer hours.
When lecturing and writing
caused schedule problems,
I would take a Saturday,
even three or four days,
without food or drink,
making up for lost prayertime.
I had splitting headaches
and insomnia for as many as five nights;
I had illness and thought I would die;
I suffered loss of my senses.
Even after recovery,
my head whirled with confusion.
God rescued me from these torrents of prayer!
Actually He had to use a little bit of force,
so captive was I to mere ritual.
Well, this has given me understanding for those
who don't buy into my teaching right away,
young theologians who don't understand
as well as I do.

John 4:38 applies to them:
    "Others have labored,
    and you have entered into
    their labors."
In St. Gregory's *Dialogues* is a story
about a studiously faithful steward
    who kept three gold pieces
        without letting his brothers know.
        He was condemned!
That's a metaphor of what I'm saying.
    When Christ is not with you,
        the devil is. He says,
            "Do it to the least detail."
    But Christ says,
        "I love you even in your mistakes."
God gives us beautiful things to generate gratitude.
    He doesn't trouble us about mistakes,
    but longtime monks don't know this.
        Munzer, Oecolampadius and Zwingli
        got out of their monasteries early,
            but they soon fell anyway.
        The devil finds "ritual" people quickly,
            especially when Christ does not
            occupy their hearts.
The devil leads one to Scripture,
    but without Christ!
He leads to law and to works!
    This means work and trouble
        before Christ helps us once more.

3. FALSE FASTING AND PRAYING

On March 20 we heard about sumptuous fasts,
    their bread and wine unlimited!

Fact is,
        just the troubled really fasted.
I myself nearly fasted to death.
Over and again I refused
even a drop of water
or a bit of food.
        I was serious!
        I crucified Christ!
        No mere observer,
        I helped carry Him,
        I pierced His hands and feet!
                God, forgive me,
                I have confessed this openly.
Here is the truth:
        The most pious monk is a rascal.
        He denies Christ as Mediator or High Priest.
        He makes Christ a judge!
Selecting twenty-one saints,
I prayed to three every day
while I celebrated mass.
        This enabled me to
        pray to all twenty-one weekly.
    I prayed most particularly to
the Blessed Virgin.
        Her feminine instincts
        took passionate care of my sins
        by appeasing her Son.
Dear me! If the Church
hadn't clobbered justification by faith,
it wouldn't have introduced
        brotherhoods,
        pilgrimages,
        masses,
        prayers to saints.

If the Church fails again
(pray God it won't),
these idols will come back.

4. *WHEN TO PRAY: WHEN NOT TO PRAY*

Someone asked
if Genesis 18:32 and Ezekiel 14:12-23
stand in conflict.
    In Genesis, God promised
    to spare Sodom
    if Abraham could find
    ten good people.
        In Ezekiel, God said that
        even if Noah prayed,
        God would turn a deaf ear.
These passages do not conflict.
        In Ezekiel,
Noah was forbidden to pray.
        In Genesis,
Abraham was not forbidden to pray.
Read the text carefully and you will learn
    that when God says,
        "Don't pray,"
            you must stop praying.
    If I say,
        "Don't pray for my nephew, Andrew,"
            but you pray anyway,
            your prayers won't help.
    But if I say,
        "Maybe someone should pray for Andrew,"
            well, that's different.
At this, someone asked,
    "How, then, do we know when God will hear our prayers?"

Normally, God doesn't tell us,
        "Don't pray."
To the contrary,
        He tells us to pray.
I would have stopped praying against the Turkish invasion
a long time ago, had God said, "Don't pray."
        But He didn't issue that command,
        so I must pray,
                even though it almost appears
                we haven't prayed at all.

5. PRAYER ACCOMPLISHES MUCH

Can someone's faith
bring salvation
for another?
        Yes, indeed!
        Just one person's faith
        can mean conversion for another.
                An example: Paul was converted
                because Stephen prayed.
But get this straight:
        Paul's faith,
        not Stephen's,
        saved him.
                Yet God honored Stephen's faith.
Because of prayer,
many still live physically.
        We prayed for Philip Melanchthon
        when he suffered terrible illness,
        and he came back to health.
        Prayer accomplishes much.
        But wasn't Paul converted
        long after Stephen's death?

No.
Paul was converted the same year.
Paul, fine, young, learned,
tried to stick to law righteousness:
 "By doing these things
 a man shall live."
  Paul saw himself pleasing God.
But God hears faith prayers,
and He acts on those prayers,
not after our patterns
but after His will.
Do you remember Augustine's mother?
 She asked God
 to save her son.
 It appears her prayers went unheard.
  She asked learned men
   to counsel Augustine.
  She asked him
   to marry a Christian girl
   so she could win him to Christ.
  That couldn't work either.
But when the Lord God came,
 He got the job done!
  Indeed, God made this man
   "a showpiece,"
  as the Church now calls him.
No wonder James asked us
 to pray for one another—
  "the prayer of a righteous person
  has great power in its effects."
   This verse, 5:16, is one
    of the best in James' epistle.
Prayer is powerful
 if one believes in it,

for God has bound Himself to it
by His promises.

6. PRAYER POWER

No one can really
know prayer's power—
    what prayer can do—
without experiencing it.
        In crisis one can lay hold on prayer.
            Earnest prayer yields a rich hearing.
                This I know from experience.
            Earnest prayer brings God Himself
                . . . in His own time.
The Book of Ecclesiasticus
    observes that the prayer
    of a good and godly person
    does more for health
    than the doctor.
        How great, upright, and godly
        the Christian's prayer!
        How powerful with God!
            Yet we face a mystery:
            A mere human can talk
            with His Majesty!
            Indeed, God smiles on us
            for Christ's sake.
    Don't let your sins or
        feelings of unworthiness
            keep you from praying.
A Bavarian went to pray
    to the idol of St. Leonard.
        Someone behind the statue said,
        "Cool it!"

The poor man stopped praying,
until one day he wised up
and talked back:
    "*You* cool it, Leonard!"
The lesson? Never listen to
    "Cool it!"
Rather, always believe God hears
when we pray with faith in Christ.
This explains the saints'
Ascensus mentis ad Deum—
    "climbing to God with your heart."
We can't understand this climbing,
but don't let language limitations
make you afraid to approach God.
    After all,
God is our strength in prayer.
    To pray conditionally
    is to pray uncertainly.
Pray with your heart,
Pray with your lips,
    for our prayers and God's love
      support the world.
Without prayer, the world
would be worse than it is.

7. NEED TEACHES US TO PRAY

Jesus put into the Lord's Prayer
everything we need.
    But without testing and frustration,
without troubles and trials,
we cannot pray right.
So God says,
    "When you get into trouble, call Me."

Without difficulties
        prayer turns into cold prattle,
        it doesn't come from your heart.
So we have a well-known proverb,
        "Need teaches us to pray."
Some say God hears *all* our words.
        St. Bernard had a different perspective:
                "God doesn't hear our words
                unless first the pray-er hears them."
Now those who have the other perspective
        torment consciences.
        Tricksters manipulate pray-ers
                so that they croak like frogs
                but benefit no one at all.
        Talk about sophistry, deception,
                fruitlessness, and counterproductivity!
Prayer is a strong wall,
Prayer is a fort of the Church.
Prayer is a divine weapon.
        And prayer is found by whom?
                By no one all alone.
                Rather, only by God's grace.
The first three petitions of
the Lord's Prayer
        take in such a range of
        great and heavenly things
        that no one can really
        comprehend them.
The fourth petition
        embraces the key to living a good life.
The fifth petition
        fights against original sin,
        and against our specific sins
                which trouble us.

Without a doubt,
    these petitions were
    penned by God Himself,
        for no mere human could
        come up with such petitions.
We can't pray
    without firm belief
    in Christ our Mediator.
    Those who don't believe this
    only mouth words.
    Even the apostles
    had something to learn.
        Jesus told them point-blank
        that they didn't pray
        as they ought.
            "Pray in My Name,"
        He instructed.
But notice their prayers
after the Holy Spirit came on them.
    Then! They prayed in His Name.
        Watch out for those
        who just speak ritual prayers,
            as if *that* met some real need.
But true pray-ers!
    Ah! those Christians
    become a strong hedge
    just like God says:
        "I looked for a man
        who would make a hedge,
        standing in the gap
        between Me and the people
            —so I wouldn't destroy them!
        But I couldn't find such a man."
Therefore, when others make a

mockery of prayer,
we must pray real prayers.
     David announced,
          "God really hears
          and acts on the prayers
          of genuinely trusting people."

8. FULFILLMENT AT DAY'S END

Daily I pray
to get my assignments done.
     And when I go to bed and
     I pray the Lord's Prayer,
          then I focus on
          two or three Scripture
          sentences.
This helps me sleep
and gives me a sense
of well-being.

9. GOD GIVES MORE THAN WE ASK

God always gives
more than we ask!
     Examples:
          Pray sincerely for bread
               and get an acre of land.
          I prayed for my ill wife,
               God not only healed her, but
               He gave us a fine farm
               and a good harvest.
My wife asked a question:
     "Why are we cold
     and careless in prayer?"

My answer:
    "The devil's always busy,
    Yet we are ice-cold
    and negligent.
        Even false worshipers
        may be diligent!"

10. PRAYER FOR RAIN—THE 1532 DROUGHT

Lord, here we are
    gathered in church
    to pray for rain.
Please keep Your promise.
    We have pleaded and sighed.
The covetous and rich farmers don't help;
    they do as they please!
        They fear nothing,
        not even death or hell.
            They make of their faith
            mere ritual.
            They have become
            haughty cutthroats.
The loan sharks among the rich
    take advantage of the people,
        and God may send punishment.
Yet, Lord, You take care of
Your own,
    But You let no
    rain
    fall on the ungodly.
Lord, through David You said,
    "The Lord is near to all
    who call on Him faithfully;
        You honor those who do Your will;

You hear their prayers.
            Those in distress You help."
Lord, why don't You give us rain?
    We have cried,
    we have prayed a long time.
Lord, Your will be done.
    Though You give no rain,
    You will give something better—
        A life
                still, quiet, peaceful.
Lord, we pray from the
bottom of our hearts:
If You will not give us rain,
the ungodly will say Christ,
the only Son, is a liar.
For He promised,
"Whatever you ask in My Name,
I will do it."

        Note: Within half an hour
        after the people left the church,
        rain came
        and lasted two weeks,
        transforming the earth.
        The rain began June 9, 1532.

11. DO PRAY FOR CONCORD

With concord
wealth increases,
    and a lot of other things
    do too.
But dissension is
dangerous and hurtful,

> most particularly in
>> the schools,
>> the noble arts,
>> the professions—
>>> just where people ought to
>>> help each other,
>>> and hug each other
>>> in loving fellowship.

To snap at one another,
to destroy each other—
> well! We can
> ruin our whole institution.

Therefore, work and pray.
> The word of faith and
> the prayers of honest people
>> are the most powerful weapons.
> Moreover, God Himself sends angels
> to surround those
> who truly honor Him.

So fight on.
> For the Lord of Hosts
> is our Commander.
>> Teach and battle.
>> Watch out!
> Our adversary pursues us.
>> Venture into the battle.
>>> Antichrist wants to win
>>> God's saints to his side,
>>> just like Daniel said.

We live in danger:
> treachery, treason,
>> money power,
>> corrupting leaders
> all threaten us.

But remember,
   an ass laden
      with money
      will do anything!

12. WHEN GOD LISTENS

Prayers from the heart,
   the sighs of poor people,
   the longings of oppressed folk—
      these set off heaven's
      alarm.
God and all angels
listen.
   Ah! God's ear is sharp;
      He knows the real thing.

13. THE DESPERATE PRAYER

Moses came to the Red Sea;
he had the Children of Israel
with him.
With tears and trembling
he prayed.
   The tears and trembling took
   no verbal expression,
      and the people took
      no notice.
Moses' plea can be translated like this:
   "O, Lord God,
   what road can I lead the people on now?
   How on earth did I get in this pickle?
   So far as I can see
   we have no way out.

Look! There's the
    Red Sea.
Look! Behind us come
    our enemies,
    the Egyptians.
Look! On both sides—
    impossible mountains.
When I look at myself,
    I'm to blame for all this."
At this point, God answered Moses:
    "Why are you so uptight?
        You've pressed the panic button;
        you've even shrieked;
            you've cried to Me very loudly;
            you've made the very heavens ring."
Well, don't try to explain all this—
    human reason can't sort it out.
        The Red Sea is broader and wider
        than the distance between
        Wittenberg and Coburg—
            in other words, 120 English miles.
More, the people had to rest at night,
    get provisions, eat their meals.
More still, we're talking about
600,000 men plus women and kids.
    Now figure how much time
    the crossing took!
    They walked by units of 150.

14. THE PRAYER GOD HEARS

Impossible!
    That God would ignore
prayers built on faith in Christ.

Not that God answers by
    the length of our prayers,
    or the way we pray,
    or the intensity of petitions.
        God will not be tied down!
But the prayers of
    the really good people,
    the transparent people—
    these prayers God hears.
        Just like St. James said:
           "Pray for one another,
           for the prayers of
           the truly righteous
           yield a great deal."

15. A POTENT PRAYER

The King of Persia
attacked
the city of Nasili.
    The Bishop of Nasili
    realized his helplessness
    against Persia.
        So he got up on the city wall,
        lifted his hands to heaven,
        and prayed
        —all this in sight of the enemy.
Well, God pestered the horses,
    covering their eyes with flies,
    countless flies stinging them.
        Riders ran away.
        God preserved the city.
Now, in just such a way
    God can save the Church

against her enemies.

16. CHRISTIANS ALWAYS PRAY

Spirit-filled Christians
   pray without stopping.
Not that they verbalize always,
   but their hearts
      live in prayer,
      both at sleep
      and during the waking hours.
      For the Christian,
      every breath, really,
      is a prayer.
One of the psalms talks about
the sighs of the poor,
and that God hears those sighs.
   Similarly,
   true Christians
always carry the cross,
      though they are not always
      fully conscious of that.

17. THE CORPORATE VALUE OF THE LORD'S PRAYER

The Lord's Prayer
binds God's people
together.
   It so knits them that
   each prays for the
   other,
      and this all at the same
      time.

So strong and powerful this
prayer
that even the fear of death
hides its face and runs.

PRAYER

Is any one of you sick? He should call the elders of the church to pray over him and anoint him with oil in the name of the Lord. And the prayer offered in faith will make the sick person well; the Lord will raise him up. If he has sinned, he will be forgiven. Therefore confess your sins to each other and pray for each other so that you may be healed. The prayer of a righteous man is powerful and effective.

James 5:14-16

HIS PRESENCE

Ask God for Himself.
His presence is preeminent.

GOD'S WORD

What is the heart of this passage?
Have you seen God at work in the life of someone who has experienced healing or some other vivid answer to prayer?

SELF-EXAMINATION

What will you do to put hands and feet to your faith?

PETITION

Pray for yourself, in light of God's message.

INTERCESSION

Now you are ready to pray for others.

FIVE

ACTIVE FAITH

1. THE TRUTH ABOUT BEING SAVED

What we believe about personal salvation
expels sorrow, and overcomes it too.
    It puts perplexities,
    unfortunate experiences
    and adversities
        into perspective.
In fact, without the knowledge
    that we are put right by faith,
        we could have neither
            help nor good counsel.
Let me give an example of what I'm talking about:
Julian the Emperor demanded that
his servants and soldiers deny Christ.
    Many refused;
    Julian murdered them.
        Would you believe

      that they died joyfully?
One of these Christians,
just a youth,
but beautifully committed,
    —well, his friends asked God
    to let him die first.
He knelt,
put his neck on the chopping block
    only to have Julian release him.
    You see, the Emperor
    wanted to test the lad
      to discover if
      his commitment
      would stick.
    You know, that young fellow
    stood to pray like this:
      "Lord, am I not worthy
      to suffer for you?"
Now! That's the faith
that overcomes death.

2. *WHAT CHRIST WANTS YOU TO DO*

Christ just wants you
to talk freely about Him.
    I know you think
    you will go blank
    and speechless.
      But remind yourself that
      Jesus invites you to call on Him
      when you get into a jam.
He promises to hear you and
give you a spirit of praise.
He says more:

That He will hear you,
be with you in trouble,
deliver you,
even bring you to honor.
The easiest work in the world
is true service to God,
to do what He commands in the Bible.
All you need do is speak up for Jesus.
But mark this:
You will suffer,
you will be humbled
with persecution.
Yet He promises
to stick with you
and to help you.

3. CONFESS CHRIST

Every Christian
—especially Church officeholders—
should be ready always
to stand up,
speak boldly, and
confess Christ as Saviour,
whenever that is required.
This readiness is a good way
to maintain your faith,
and to keep your weaponry up-to-date
against sectarianism,
the devil,
all evil.
Here's the clincher:
Everyone can do this
when faith is active.

By this I mean:
    Be sure of your beliefs,
    be certain of your practices.
You see, God doesn't change,
    So if you change,
    you're in trouble.
        Why go down the tubes?
          Anchor yourself
          to the Rock of Gibralter.

4. REASON CANNOT COMPREHEND GOD'S WORKS

Look at everything,
    even the least of God's creatures.
      Such works!
Which of us—
    even the very smart,
    the very wise,
    the very saintly—
        can make a fig tree
        out of a single fig,
          or indeed create
          just another fig?
Which of us
        can make a cherry tree
        out of a cherry seed,
          or indeed create
          just another cherry?
Which of us
        can know how God produces
        and preserves all things
          and causes them to grow?
Truly we see the imprint of the Trinity

on all art and creation:
    the power of God
        the Father,
    the wisdom of God
        the Son,
    the goodness of God
        the Spirit.
But don't try to understand any of this.
    Who can create
        an eye that sees?
    Who can tell how words
        formed on the tongue
        and shaped by the mouth
            get through to another mind?
    Who can know
        how any natural thing works?
            We see these phenomena daily,
            but know little about them.
Don't be surprised, then,
that you cannot know God's secrets,
even by lots of research.
    Sense,
        wit,
            reason,
                understanding—
none of our powers of knowing
can plow the depths of God's works.

5. OUR INABILITY TO UNDER-STAND GOD'S CREATIVITY

No one can imagine—
    much less understand—
        what God did and continues to do.

Suppose we labored with
    blood, sweat, and tears
    to write just three lines
    like St. John penned.
        We could never pull it off.
Why, then, should we take
pride in our wisdom,
or wonder at our lack of wisdom?
    I for one accept myself
    just as I am,
        a fool imprisoned
        by my limitations.
People ask where God
lived
before heaven.
        St. Augustine answered
        that God lived
        just in Himself.
Someone else asked me
the same question.
        I answered that God
        was building hell
        for idle questioners!
After God created everything,
    He was everywhere,
    yet nowhere,
        certainly I can't
        get close to God
            without His Word.
        But He allows Himself
        to be found
            in His Word.
        Jews found Him in Jerusalem
            at His throne of grace.

We find Him in the Word
        at baptism,
        in Holy Communion,
        in faith.
But in His Majesty,
        in His Holy otherness,
        we cannot find Him.
In the Old Testament
    He, by special grace,
allowed Himself to be
found in specific places:
        in the tabernacle at Shiloh,
            Shechem, and Gibeon;
        in the temple at Jerusalem.
Greeks tried to make divinity
local to cities and temples:
    Diana at Ephesus,
Apollo at Delphos.
        Notice that where
        God builds a church,
        the devil also
        builds a temple.
            These pagan places
            imitate
            Jewish houses of worship:
            Because God is hidden,
            pagans make dark places;
            the devil only apes God.
But God does not
reveal Himself
by mere imitation;
        He makes Himself known
            through Christ,
            the Word, and faith.

6. GOD'S GENEROSITY

What if God would
        halt the shining of the sun,
        lock up the air,
        detain the water,
        quench the fire!
                We would give all
                our money and resources
                to restore nature.
But God heaps His gifts on us liberally.
        We claim them as our right!
        God would not dare cripple nature!
But why should we allow God's generosity
to make our faith inactive?
                Even the ungodly
                ought to recognize God
                in His gifts.

7. THE INVITATION TO TRUST

One evening two birds
        flew into my garden
        and made a nest.
I invited the birds to stay:
        "I'm very happy
        with you
        in my garden.
                Trust me;
                I won't harm you."
But sometimes,
                in the days that followed,
                passersby scared
                the birds away.

We are like those untrusting birds,
    yet God always treats us kindly;
      He takes care of us.

8. GOD TAKES CARE OF US

God's great power nourishes
and maintains the whole world.
    Nonetheless, we find difficulty
    in really embracing
    the clause in the Creed,
       "I believe in God the Father."
But look at the facts:
    God created all things;
    these things meet all our needs:
       we fish the seas;
       we hunt in the woods;
       we mine silver and gold;
       we harvest fruit;
       we gather wheat;
         the earth is our pantry.

9. GOD, NOT MONEY, PRESERVES THE WORLD

God, not wealth,
preserves and maintains the world.
    Riches make people
    proud and lazy.
The wealthiest people live in Venice.
    But recently in trouble,
    these Venetians went for help
    to the Turks,
    who sent twenty-four galleys of wheat.

But as the Turks approached the city,
    the ships sank;
all the wheat went into the sea
    as the people of Venice watched!
Wealth can't
stop hunger;
    but wealth
    can cause hunger.
        Where money abounds,
        prices go up.
            Money cannot bring
            true happiness;
    Jesus saw money
    as thorns
    which prick people.
        Yet people
        still think money
        can make them happy.

10. COWS AND SHEEP ARE PREACHERS

One evening
while the cows and sheep
were coming in from pasture,
I exclaimed,
    "There go preachers:
        givers of milk,
        givers of butter,
        givers of cheese,
        givers of wool."
Every day these animals
tell us something:
    put faith in God;
    trust in God who looks after us.

Believe in our loving Father who
    attends to us,
    keeps us,
    provides for
    our every need.

11. GOD CARES FOR ANIMALS TOO

No one can calculate
God's care
of animals in nature.
    I am sure
    God's expenditure,
    just for sparrows,
        comes to more than
        the annual revenue
        of the King of France.

12. GOD HONORS THE HUMBLE

All who are truly humble before God,
    take a tremendous step forward.
    To all the unpretentious,
        God can be only kind.
If God were only stern and angry,
    I'd be afraid of Him!
        God's enemies (the tyrants) put fear into me,
        but God takes fear out of me.

13. DISCIPLINE, GOD'S INSTRUMENT

God acts where He finds good discipline.
    A settled government
    comes with discipline.

            Otherwise things
            fall apart.
The wisdom of the wise
disintegrates without controls;
the wise become
mad in their procedures.
Look at the sea:
        There are boundaries
        to contain the beating, raging waves.
            Otherwise the water
            would overrun and cover everything.
        God defines the compass of the water,
            not with iron
                but with walls of sand.

14. LET GOD BE GOD

Plato talked about God as *nothing*, yet
said He is all things.
        Dr. Eck and the Sophists
        also said things about
        God
        no one can understand.
But God is invisible
and incomprehensible;
        so what we see
        or comprehend—
            that is not God.
Let me share another perspective:
        God is visible
        in His Word and works.
            But don't even desire
            to find Him anyplace
            but in His Word and works.

He will be found
only
where He reveals
Himself.
People who attempt
to find Him elsewhere—
in speculations—
find not God
but the devil,
who becomes to them a god,
for the devil *will* become a god!
Now hear this:
Avoid such speculations,
avoid flying too high,
stay close to the manger,
stay by the swaddling clothes
—the Scriptures—
wherein Christ lies.
St. Paul says that in Christ
the fullness of God dwells.
Focus on Christ.
In Him you cannot miss God.

Active Faith

I am not ashamed of the Gospel, because it is the power of God for the salvation of everyone who believes: first for the Jew, then for the Gentile. For in the Gospel a righteousness from God is revealed, a righteousness that is by faith from first to last, just as it is written: "The righteous will live by faith."

Romans 1:16-17

HIS PRESENCE

Ask God for Himself.
His presence is preeminent.

GOD'S WORD

In your own words, summarize the verses above.
What is the heart of this passage?
Do you know someone who lives by these verses?

SELF-EXAMINATION

What is the good news for you in these verses?
What sin, now uncovered, must you confess?
What will you do to put hands and feet to your faith?

PETITION

Pray for yourself, in light of God's message.

INTERCESSION

Now you are ready to pray for others.

SIX

PREACHERS AND PREACHING

1. APOSTOLIC PREACHING

After Christ's resurrection,
the apostles preached powerfully
through the whole world.
> By then He had sent the Holy Spirit
> who worked through the apostles,
> showing Christ's teachings clearly.
>> That preaching produced more fruit
>> than when Christ preached!
>> And you remember what Christ said,
>>> "Those who believe in Me
>>> will do the works that I do,
>>> and even greater works."
Christ might have forced
truth into people,
but He chose rather to let His
powerful preaching come gently.

After all,
giving up the rituals
of Jewish worship—
    that kind of change
    came the hard way.

2. GOD SUPPLIES THE PREACHER'S NEEDS

Jesus preached without wages,
yet God met His needs.
    He delivered and healed some women
    who ministered to him.
        Note not only that they supplied Him,
        but that He took what they offered,
        He received it willingly and gladly.
When Jesus sent the apostles to preach,
He told them,
    "Freely you have received,
    freely give."
He told them not to take anything with them,
        not to worry about food and clothing.
          "Wherever you go,
          people will take care of you."

3. THE GOSPEL DOES GET THROUGH

Such a wonder
that the Gospel gets through to people,
despite the Church!
    The Church can get pretty
    law oriented,
    pretty rule centered.
Yet God wonderfully preserves His Gospel
in the Church.

Look at pulpits now:
 Preachers teach the Gospel,
 word for word.
  The Creed,
  the Lord's Prayer,
  intercession,
  baptism,
  the Lord's Supper—
 all stay with the Church
 in the hearts of the people,
 in spite of bad leadership.
God awakens spiritual and knowledgeable persons
 to reveal His Word;
 God gives these preachers courage
  to cry out against false teachings
  and abuses that creep into the Church.
  John Huss is an example
  of such a courageous preacher.

4. PREACH JUST CHRIST

Christ desires only this:
 "Preach Him."
You argue:
 "When I preach only Him,
 words freeze on my lips."
Pay no attention to those feelings;
just remember Christ's promises:
  "Ask and you shall receive",
  "I will deliver you,
  and bring you honor";
   "Call on Me in trouble,
   and I will hear you,
   and you shall praise Me."

With all those promises,
how could our work be easier?
    Christ loads us with light assignments;
    He only asks belief in Him;
    He only asks that we preach Him.
True, you will suffer persecution for this.
But even in this He promises:
      "I will be with you in trouble,
      I will help you."
I make no such promise to my servant
when he goes to work in the garden
or when he goes shopping for me.
    But Christ promises to
    meet my every need!
Here's the problem:
    We fail in belief.
    Yet scriptural faith can do anything!
      But I'm weak, and so
      I must rest in Christ's words to Paul:
        "My grace is sufficient for you,
        for my power is strong in weakness."

5. PRACTICE, DON'T SPECULATE

The proof of the pudding
lies in putting truth to practice,
    not in speculation or
    spinning "great" ideas.
      Those who speculate
      rather than practice,
      either in household matters
      or in government circles,
      only prove that their ideas don't work.
Suppose a businessman

shows a profit,
but can't make his product work.
He may talk big about the product,
but people who buy it can't work it.
Boy! is his day of reckoning coming.
So it is with speculating preachers,
the kind we see to this day.

6. THE TWOFOLD NATURE OF A CALL

Do nothing unless called.
And how do we know when we're called?
Two ways:
God's voice heard by faith;
a friend's request
to which we respond out of love,
as when a fellow minister
asks us to preach for him.
In order to keep a clear conscience,
respond to both kinds of call.

7. SOMETIMES GOD CALLS THROUGH PERCEIVED NEED

Young people must learn the Scriptures.
When they know the Bible and
when they possess gifts for preaching,
they may offer their services like this:
A church needs a pastor,
but the young person must
wait for an invitation.
A young woman
wants to get married,
but *she* doesn't propose;

be does that.
Then she feels good about
marrying the young man,
and everybody else
feels good about it too.
One may, of course, indicate willingness:
"If you want me,
I'll serve."
That attitude documents the possibility
of an authentic service opportunity.
Isaiah said,
"Here am I;
send me."
Isaiah offered himself
when he saw the need
for a preacher.
The bottom line:
When we see a need,
when the people want us—
well, that can lead to a call.

8. LONG, DRY SERMONS!

Don't torment your hearers;
don't keep them sitting in church
with long, tedious sermons.
Such preaching robs the pulpit of delight;
people stop listening;
preachers hurt themselves.

9. MOSES AND I PREACH RELUCTANTLY

God had to talk to Moses several times
before he would go preach.

Moses presented excuses,
but finally went, unwillingly.
Had I been in Moses' shoes,
I would have hired a lawyer
to frame a complaint against God.
God seemed to have broken His promise.
"I will be with you," He assured,
but God seemed to renege.
That's the way with us too.
God promises,
"You shall find rest for your souls."
But look at John the Baptist,
see what happened to Jesus,
notice the martyrs,
observe your own experience.
If we took all this to lawyers,
God would lose.
Christ spoke to me as He spoke to Paul:
"Get up and preach,
and I will be with you."
But preaching Christ
puts me in danger!
Had I known then
what I now know,
I would have opted out,
Yet with Moses I must say,
"Send whom you will send."

10. HELP THE WEAK, CAUTION THE ERRING?

What is preferable?
To lift the weak or
to caution adversaries?

Both are good and necessary,
but helping the weak is preferable.
	Notice, however, that when you
	put those led astray on their guard,
	you also help the immature.
Both callings are God's gifts.
	If you excel in teaching,
		get busy and teach;
	if you do best at warning people,
		see to that.

11. THE SECRET OF POWERFUL PREACHING

What is the secret of
the art of powerful preaching?
The first commandment:
	"I am the Lord your God."
		God is firm and unbending
			towards bad people;
		God is kind and merciful
			towards good people.
This explains why we preach
		hellfire to the proud and haughty,
		paradise to the godly;
		reproof to the wicked,
		comfort to the good.
	We have different tools on our workbenches.
		Some knives cut better than others.
		The sermons
		of Dr. Cordatus
		and Dr. Cruciger
		get to hearts better
		than the preaching of others.

12. *INDICATORS OF A GOOD PREACHER*

A good preacher
    teaches systematically,
    has a ready wit,
    articulates well,
    speaks with a good voice,
    possesses a good memory,
    exercises terminal facilities,
    feels secure in doctrine,
    invests everything,
        even life and possessions,
        in the Word,
    suffers willingly
        jeering and mockery
        from everybody.

13. *CLEAR AWAY PROBLEMS!*

People notice defects immediately!
    A preacher can have ten good qualities,
    but if he has even one fault,
    that eclipses the ten virtues.
        That's a commentary on the world.
A case study: Dr. Justus Jonas.
    He has all the virtues
    and qualities a preacher could possess.
        But alas! His behavior:
        He hums and spits.
            Result?
            Though he is a good
            and an honest man,
            people can't stand him.

14. DISCERNMENT

A preacher needs to know
how to tell the difference between
the impenitent and the secure in God,
the sorrowing and the penitent,
    Otherwise the Scriptures don't unlock themselves.
Case study: Amsdorf preaching
    to the princes of Schmalcalden.
    He preached with great earnestness,
    announcing that the Gospel belongs
        to the poor,
        to the sorrowing.
    The Gospel has a hard time getting through
        to princes, to great persons,
        to courtiers
        who live without hardship.

15. CLERGY AND LAITY

Ongoing hatred of laity for clergy
is not without reason.
    Unbridled people
    of both upper and lower strata
    don't like censure.
Here's the challenge to clergy:
    Preachers must expose sinners;
        they break the Commandments
          of both tablets.
    Yet, reproof doesn't come to
    their ears comfortably,
        and that's why they
        look at preachers
        with a critical eye.

16. A LESSON IN PUBLIC PREACHING

Speak with intentionality,
and speak unhurriedly.
   This delivery style
   communicates with effect
   and lasting impact.
Seneca writes of Cicero,
   "He speaks intentionally
      from his heart."

17. SPEAK SIMPLY AND DIRECTLY

Plug into your hearers
right where they are.
   Most preachers fail just here,
   they preach above the heads
   of poor, simple people.
Plain understandable preaching is a great art.
   Christ Himself talks about
   tilling the ground,
   mustard seed,
   sheep.
      His metaphors
      come out of daily life,
      simplicity is their trademark.

18. HANDLING FEAR OF PEOPLE

Most preachers get into the pulpit
   and suffer a kind of paralysis
      because of all those heads out there.
      I don't see heads,
      I see blocks!

19. *USE YOUR MOTHER TONGUE*

Preachers should not use Hebrew,
    Greek, or other foreign languages.
        We must talk in church
        like we do at home,
        in the unvarnished mother tongue.
            Everyone identifies with that!
Let the courtiers and lawyers
    and other sophisticated people
        employ unusual and ear-catching words.
Dr. Staupitz is a learned man;
    he is also irksome.
People would rather hear
    a plain preacher
    they can comprehend.
Church is no place to parade your ego.
    St. Paul never talked like
    Demosthenes and Cicero;
        he used appropriate and plain words,
        shaping language to make it
            meaningful to his people.

20. *THE HUMILITY OF THE HYPOCRITES*

The humility of the hypocrites
is really the haughtiest pride.
    The Pharisee who "humbled" himself
    and gave God thanks
    showed his true colors:
        "I'm not like others,
        nor like this publican."
Self-flatterers see only themselves as wise;
    they throw out the opinions of all others;

they accept only what pleases them.

21. AMBITION

The rankest poison to the church?
        Ambition!
When it takes possession of preachers,
ambition becomes a consuming fire.
    But Scripture aims to destroy
    the desires of the flesh.
        Don't seek honor.
            My! What people get proud about!
            Born in sin, every moment
            we live in danger of death.
        What are we proud about?
            Our scabs?
            Our weaknesses?
            Our uncleanness?

22. HONOR?

Homer,
Virgil,
Terence
        could get away with honor-seeking,
            but you don't find that
                in Holy Scripture.
        Christ says,
            "Hallowed be Your Name,
            Yours be the glory"
                —not ours.
        Christ charges us,
            "Preach the Word of God."
The world will see us preachers

as fools and unworthy;
that opens the door
for God to be seen as
>   just,
>   wise,
>   merciful.
>   That's the nature of God;
>   no one else is perfect like that.
When we honor God for who He is,
when we let His kingdom be just that,
when we acknowledge His will,
>   then He gives us everything we need,
>   then He picks up the bill for our sins,
>   then He delivers us from all evil,
>   then He protects us from the devil.
Honor?
>   Only God can have it.

23. *REALITY AND LAZINESS*

At my advanced age
I would like rest and peace,
>   but those who ought to be on my side
>   oppose me.
The usual adversaries plague me enough,
>   but my own brothers do too!
>   I can't do much about this;
>   these opponents—
>   unwilted youth,
>   chomping at the bit—
>   live in idleness.
I'm old now—
>   with a lot of hard work under my belt,
>   and pains too.

Case study: Osiander.
    His pride swells with idle living.
        He preaches only two times a week,
            but enjoys an income
            of 400 guilders annually!

24. OUR EPICUREAN LISTENERS

For the most part,
our listeners are Epicureans.
    They measure our preaching in terms
    of how they would like to live—easily.
Pharisees and Sadducees
were Christ's enemies,
yet they listened to Him.
    Why?
        The Pharisees listened to catch Him,
        the Sadducees listened to discredit Him.
The Pharisees are the friars today;
the Sadducees are the nice people.
    They look like listeners,
    they pretend to believe our preaching,
    but go on doing what pleases them.
    The bottom line:
        They remain Epicureans.

25. HOW TO GET THROUGH
TO YOUR PEOPLE

Preachers must know how to sequence material,
    they must know how to really get through.
Furthermore, preachers must be able to teach,
    and know how
    to turn on caution lights.

When preachers address a concern,
they must do the following:
    First, bring the concern into clear focus.
    Second, define the concern visually,
        and then make it walk
            so everybody sees it in action.
    Third, show that the concern is scriptural,
        thus giving it authority.
    Fourth, give examples to explain it
        and thus emblazon it on minds.
    Fifth, make it aesthetic
        with similes and metaphors.
    Sixth, warn the unaware,
        wake up the sleepy,
        shake up the disobedient, the heretics,
            and the authors of bad ideas.
But these warnings must come not
    from hatred or envy,
        but to honor God
    and for the rewards that come
        with saved and healthy people.

26. PREACHING ITSELF IS A TEACHER

Preaching teaches me about
    the world, the flesh,
    the malignity of the devil.
        We could know none of these things
        without the Gospel revealed and
        without preaching the Gospel.
My confession:
    Until I preached the Gospel
    I thought there were only two sins:
        Self-indulgence and sexual promiscuity.

27. ST. PAUL THE PREACHER

Paul understood the Old Testament
better than anyone else. Of course,
    there was John the Baptist,
    there was John the Divine,
    there was Peter too.
        St. Matthew and others
        did well with Old Testament history,
        and that's very necessary.
            But none of these writers seemed
            to grasp the Old Testament
            like St. Paul did.
St. Paul translated a lot of Hebrew into Greek,
others couldn't do it like he did.
    In a single chapter
    he could summarize half a dozen
    Old Testament chapters.
    Observe how he loved
        Moses, Isaiah, and David.
        David
        Paul got his theology
        from the prophets.
Well now, you young preachers:
    Study Hebrew and Greek
    so you can compare
    Old and New Testament words.
        This way you can become
        a detective of Scripture,
        sorting out its traits,
        personality, and energy.

PREACHERS AND PREACHING

How, then, can they call on the One they have not believed in? And how can they believe in the One of whom they have not heard? And how can they hear without someone preaching to them? And how can they preach unless they are sent? . . . Consequently, faith comes from hearing the message, and the message is heard through the word of Christ.

Romans 10:14-17

HIS PRESENCE

Ask God for Himself.
His presence is preeminent.

GOD'S WORD

What is the heart of this passage?
Do you know a preacher who lives by these verses?

SELF-EXAMINATION

What is the good news for you in these verses?
What sin, now uncovered, must you confess?
What will you do to put hands and feet to your faith?

PETITION

Pray for yourself, in light of God's message.

INTERCESSION

Now you are ready to pray for others.

SEVEN

SIN

1. SINS

No Church Father talked much about sin
    until Augustine, who showed the difference
       between original and actual sin.
    Original sin is this:
       To covet,
       to lust,
       to grasp greedily after things,
          a desire pattern
          which is the root cause
          of actual sin.
    These desires come to Christians
          but God forgives them
          for Jesus' sake,
    and Christians resist bad desires
    by the help of the Holy Spirit.

Some oppose this clear truth about sin.
>St. Paul cries out to sinners
>who reject red warning flags;
>>such carelessness means self-condemnation.
>Jesus says,
>>"Leave these heedless sinners alone;
>>they are blind leaders of the blind."
If someone makes a mistake through ignorance,
>instruction can bring correction.
>But one who has a hardened heart
>and will not face the truth is like Pharaoh
>>who would not acknowledge his sins;
>>he would not humble himself before God,
>>>and met his doom at the Red Sea.
We are all sinners by nature.
>We were conceived in sin,
>>born in sin,
>>poisoned by sin through and through.
We have received from Adam
>a will set against God
>until the Holy Spirit
>>changes and revitalizes us.
Philosophers and lawyers
can't help us theologically,
>because they don't know all this.
>>They don't develop their value systems
>>>from God's Word.

2. SINS AGAINST THE HOLY SPIRIT

What are these sins?
>First, being too sure of yourself.
>Second, allowing yourself to become a defeatist.
>Third, out-and-out opposing of known truth.

Fourth, wishing someone ill will
    instead of goodwill,
and thus discouraging that person
    from saying yes to God's grace.
Fifth, having a hardened heart.
Sixth, being unrepentant.

3. THE SIN AGAINST GOD'S WORD

We have inside us many sins.
    Examples:
        Anger.
        Impatience.
        Wanting what belongs to others.
        Greed.
        Ungoverned appetites.
        Hate.
        Antagonism.
    All these God sees as big sins;
    the whole world suffers nonstop from them.
But one sin is bigger:
    Crying out against God's Word.
        Think about this:
        Not one of the sins listed above
        could be committed
            if we would love
            and respect God's Word.
But alas!
    The entire world drowns in this sin.
        No one gives a fig for the Gospel;
        all growl at it;
        all martyr it;
    all claim,
        "This attitude is no sin."

Observe churchgoers:
    One looks this way,
    another looks that way;
    few come really to listen.
        Such a common sin!
        People never see it as they see other sins.
    Such a "little sin,"
        they say.
    "Why do we need to pay attention so diligently?
    Why do we need
        to mark, learn,
        and inwardly digest the sermon?"
Other sins strike us differently.
    Killing someone,
    sleeping with someone,
    taking what is not ours;
        these sins bring grief,
        sorrow in our memory banks,
        and remorse.
But inattention to God's Word,
    condemning it,
    persecuting it,
        —that's unrecognized sin.
The result: a really frightening situation.
    Land and people will destruct
    just as Jerusalem, Rome,
    Greece, and other kingdoms
    went through destruction.

4. CHRIST'S EVALUATION

Christ knew how to distinguish sins.
    The Gospels show Him harsh to Pharisees;
        they hated Him and His Word.

He took a gentle and warm attitude
   toward the woman who sinned.
We see the same contrast today:
   Envy robs Christ of His Word;
     He stands resolutely
     against that attitude
      and shoots it down.
But the woman—the "greatest" sinner—
   grasps His Word,
   listens to Christ,
   washes His feet with expensive cologne,
     and believes that He alone
     can save the world.

5. FORGIVENESS

God forgives sins by grace
for Christ's sake.
   But we dare not abuse that grace.
Note God's vehicles for communicating forgiveness:
   Gospel preaching, baptism,
   the Lord's Prayer,
   the Holy Spirit in us.
We must document our own forgiveness by this:
   Forgiving the faults of others.
      And don't start comparing,
        for what's 100 pennies
        compared to $10,000?
      We deserve nothing because we forgive;
        we must forgive because
        this proves God forgives us.
God's Word announces forgiveness of sins;
   in His Word only we find this truth;
     its supporting beams are God's promises.

Why does God forgive sins?
    Not because we feel them,
    nor because we sorrow over them,
    not because we deserve forgiveness,
        but because He is merciful.
        He forgives us because of Christ.

6. TWO DEADLY SINS

Tricky, these two sins—hate and pride!
    They deck themselves,
    trim themselves,
    clothe themselves
        to look like God.
    Hate parades itself as holy.
    Pride parades itself as truth.
        But this pair of sins leads to death:
            Hate kills.
            Pride lies.

7. OUT WITH IT—CONFESS YOUR SIN!

No one gets hurt
    acknowledging and confessing sins.
So you have committed a sin.
    Face it.
    In God's Name don't deny it,
    but from your heart say,
        "O Lord God!
        I did this bad thing."
You may not have committed
    this or that sin,
    but you have committed another.
    It's easy to say,

> "He did this sin,
>> she did that sin,"
>>> to escape owning up
>>> to your own sin!

A parable: The Seller of Young Wolves.
The customer asks, "Will you point out the best wolves?"
The seller answers falsely, "If one's good, so's another.
They are all alike."
If you have murdered, slept around,
developed into an alcoholic,
>> —well, I've blasphemed
>> by false worship.
>>> I wish I'd sinned another way,
>>> but what is done is done.
>>> He who has stolen,
>>> let him steal no more.

8. LIKE A WOUND ALWAYS HEALING

Original sin after conversion
is like a wound starting to heal.
>> It is a wound,
>> it is healing,
>> it is a sore and it runs.

So original sin stays in Christians till death,
>> yet it is dying and
>> its head is smashed,
>>> so it cannot make them hopeless.

9. INFECTED MOTIVES

All natural inclinations show
>> the absence of God or opposition to God.
>> That's why none of us is truly good.

Proof?
>   All our likes,
>   all our desires,
>   all our leanings
>   —all these are evil, wicked, spoiled.
> The Scripture says this.
> Experience documents this too:
>   No man is the perfect father,
>   loving his children faultlessly
>   and bringing them up
>   to follow only God.
>   No man is the flawless hero,
>   motivated only by the common good.
>   He possesses personal ambition
>   and that gets him into trouble.
>   This means wicked native motivations.
> But God!
>   He's patient with our motivations;
>   He somehow overlooks them
>   when we believe in Christ.

10. RIGHT PERSPECTIVE

Scheneck preaches on sin
>   in a monstrous way,
>   haranguing without discernment.
> I myself listened to him
>   from the pulpit at Eisenach.
>   With no qualification he said,
>   "Sin is nothing;
>   God takes in sinners;
>   He tells us they will
>   enter heaven's kingdom."
> Scheneck does not show the difference between

past sins,
present sins,
future sins.
    So people believe they can sin:
        "Doesn't God accept sinners?
        So let's sin."
This teaching is just plain wrong.
    When God promises to take in sinners,
        He means *repenting* sinners.

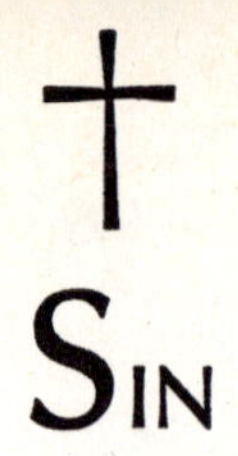

Sin

He who does what is right is righteous, just as He is righteous. He who does what is sinful is of the devil, because the devil has been sinning from the beginning. The reason the Son of God appeared was to destroy the devil's work. No one who is born of God will continue to sin, because God's seed remains in him. He cannot go on sinning, because he has been born of God. This is how we know who the children of the devil are: Anyone who does not do what is right is not a child of God; neither is anyone who does not love his brother. 1 John 3:7-10

HIS PRESENCE

Ask God for Himself.
His presence is preeminent.

GOD'S WORD

What is the heart of this passage?

SELF-EXAMINATION

What is the good news for you in these verses?

PETITION

Pray for yourself, in light of God's message.

INTERCESSION

Now you are ready to pray for others.

EIGHT

FREE WILL

1. FREE WILL WITHOUT GOD'S GRACE

St. Augustine writes like this about free will
aside from God's grace and Spirit:
    "We can only sin!"
    That bothers the scholars; they say:
        "Augustine spoke mere hyperbole.
        Augustine exaggerated.
        Augustine takes out of context
        the passages about every imagination
        of the heart being evil."
But we must conclude that indeed
    without grace and God's Spirit
    people can only sin nonstop,
        falling from one sin into another.
That's what happens when they
    ignore sound teaching and say no
        to the Word that can save them through and through.

That's what happens when they
    resist the Holy Spirit,
        and by their own wills fight God.
This means blasphemy, lusts, and selfish desires.
    And all history documents this.
An essential assignment:
    Ponder Moses' thought about
        imaginations:
        they stem from our memories and
        are all infected with evil.
    This means our invented thoughts,
    frames of reference, free wills, and noblest efforts
        are all bathed in evil always.
    Put another way,
        without God's Spirit,
        reason, will, and understanding
            prevent us from having true knowledge.
    But without true knowledge,
        we walk in the dark and embrace the worst
        as if it were the best.
I'm referring to spiritual matters as the Bible does,
    differentiating between
    secular and spiritual things
        —politics and theology.
God permits ungodly governments to exist,
    even rewards their good works,
    but He limits all this to earth.
        We fool ourselves if we
            assume the obvious and temporary
            to be actually good,
            even the supreme good.
When we theologians refer to free will,
    we want to know what it accomplishes
        for God and for *eternal* good.

Our conclusion?
    God sees us as wicked through and through,
        even if we look like a million dollars,
        even if we possess fine social skills,
        even if we observe the work ethic.
Documentation for this conclusion?
    Why, look at the unconverted
    with their morality,
    moderation, fidelity,
    love of country, parents, spouses, kids,
        stoutheartedness,
        largeheartedness,
        and liberality.
But their natural inclinations about
    God and worship and divine will
        come up blind and black.
Why?
        Their "enlightened" understanding,
        unique to human beings,
        sees good only in terms of profit.
True,
    certain non-Christian thinkers
        glimpsed the true God and genuine wisdom.
That's why some people see
        Socrates
        Xenephon,
        Plato, and
        others as prophets.
But they cannot see Christ
as the sinner's Saviour.
        Yes, their speeches sound
        beautiful, noble, and wise,
            but their souls are sightless
            and unaware.

2. *GOD'S WILL BEFORE MY WILL*

The Church Fathers did not like
the expression *free will*.
    But I believe God gave us free will.
    A question:
        Where does the power to choose
        come from?
Notice the characteristics of *our* free will:
    Subversive
    unruly
    unfaithful
    wishy-washy.
    Clearly, only God can work in us
        to do good,
and we must surrender to that.
        He is like a potter,
            we like clay.
        What *He* wills gives us freedom
        to go through pain and to work.
Freedom, as we imagine it,
        is not in us,
        because of our inability
            to do anything truly good.

3. *OUR HELPLESSNESS, BUT GOD'S POWER*

I find myself resolving to
    live right,
    lead a genuinely godly life,
    stop anything that hinders that life.
        But like Peter, who promised
        to die for Christ,
        I don't follow through.

I refuse to lie,
I won't hide from the truth,
I openly confess that I can't do good,
    even though I want to,
    but must just wait
        for God to give me grace.
Our will swings from ego-tripping—"I can do anything"—
    to ego-clobbering—"I can do nothing."
No human being can keep the Law perfectly.
    Law dialogues with me like this:
        Law: "I am grand, elevated,
            steep like a mountain you must climb."
        My Free Will: "Sure I'll climb the mountain!"
        My Second Thoughts: "I can't climb that mountain.
            I'm helpless. I won't even try."
There you have it:
    Ego-tripping and ego-clobbering.
    Yet we must preach the law
        and teach it too,
        for if we don't,
            people get rude and become smart alecs.
    When we preach the law,
        people stand in awe of it.

4. BOAST OF FREE WILL?

O Lord God!
    How could we boast of our free will?
        As though it could do any small thing,
            any divine thing, any spiritual thing?
All we need do is consider the
    horrendous adversities the devil
        introduced to us through sin
            . . . enough to shame us to our graves!

Free will brought us original sin and death,
 then troubles of all kinds like we see daily:
  murder,
  lying,
  deception,
  stealing,
   so that all of us
   are robbed of security.
 In a split second we can suffer
  loss of body or of possessions.
  We all live in danger.
We can't really know how people changed
 after the fall of our original parents,
  because we have inherited so much.
 We must characterize ourselves as
  full of puzzles and untrusting,
  poisoned physically
  and in our personalities too.
   Every part of us suffers corruption.
So my position is this:
 Anyone who thinks that by free will
 he can do anything
  says no to Christ.
I've always taken this position in my writings,
 especially against Erasmus,
  one of the world's most learned scholars.
I stand resolutely by my thesis
because I know it is true;
 I will stand by it
 even if all the world opposes it.
  Divine truth stands
  against hell's gates.
Sure, we have free will,
 but its function is to milk cows and build houses.

Beyond this, free will is helpless.
When we enjoy nonstressful living,
safety, and all we need,
we suppose we have free will.
But let need appear—
the lack of food, drink, money—
then where's free will?
It collapses in the pinch.
What does stand in the pinch is faith.
It is sure, for it seeks Christ.
You see, then, how different
faith and free will really are.
Free will equals a zero,
faith equals all that's good.
Do you think your free will
possesses courage and holding power
in an epidemic,
in war or famine?
No! Let an epidemic come
and fear will paralyze you.
You will want to go hide many miles away.
Let famine come and you will wonder
where to find something to eat.
In such times
your will cannot help you.
The more you try
the weaker you get.
You look like a leaf
shaking in the wind.
Such "valiant" things
your free will achieves!

FREE WILL

One day Jesus was praying in a certain place. When He finished, one of His disciples said to Him, "Lord, teach us to pray, just as John taught his disciples." He said to them, "When you pray, say: 'Father, hallowed be Your name, Your kingdom come. Give us each day our daily bread. Forgive us our sins, for we also forgive everyone who sins against us. And lead us not into temptation.' "   Luke 11:1-4

HIS PRESENCE

Ask God for Himself.
His presence is preeminent.

GOD'S WORD

What is the heart of this passage?
Do you know someone who lives by faith and by God's will?

SELF-EXAMINATION

What is the good news for you in these verses?
What sin, now uncovered, must you confess?
What will you do to put hands and feet to your faith?

PETITION

Pray for yourself, in light of God's message.

INTERCESSION

Now you are ready to pray for others.

NINE

ANGELS

1. WHAT IS AN ANGEL?

An angel is
    a spiritual creature without a body,
      made by God for service
        to Christians and the Church.

2. HOW TO TEACH ABOUT ANGELS

Talk about angels.
    The Church needs to be
    aware of angels.
      God's preachers should do
      an orderly job
      of teaching about angels.
First, define angels as spiritual and without bodies.
Second, teach what kind of spirits angels are:
    They're good, not bad.

Take time to discuss evil spirits.
God did not make them evil,
they got that way by rebelling.
This hatred of Christ
started in Paradise,
and will continue
until the world ends.
Third, indicate the function of angels.
They model humility in that they serve us,
even though we are imperfect
and they are perfect.
They serve us in our homes,
in society, in Church matters,
in menial tasks
some people are ashamed to do.
They serve us with integrity and faithfulness.
So this is the way to teach about angels.
And we must do it carefully and methodically,
zeroing in on their sweet and loving ways.
To teach about angels
in a disorderly manner
really helps no one.

3. ANGELS PROTECT US

Angels have long arms!
They protect those for whom
God puts out a command,
so that the devil cannot hurt us.
Angels live in God's presence,
yet they help even us.
When the devil aims to harm us,
the angels stop him
and drive him away.

Angels live with God and His Son, Christ;
    yet, they are very close to us;
        they even surround us
            while we do God's assignments.
The devil is near and around us,
    forever following us,
        trying to rob us of Life,
            health, and salvation.
But God's angels defend us!
    They stop Satan
        from doing the bad things
        he would like to do.

4. NO DOUBT ABOUT IT!
ABSOLUTELY NONE

It's a good thing
    we don't really know
        how hard angels fight;
        the battle's a rough go!
If we knew how many angels fight a single devil,
    we would lose hope.
Thus the brevity of Scripture on angels:
    "He assigns His angels
        to take charge of you.
    The Lord's angel camps all
        around those who respect God."
So then, all you who respect God,
    take courage, don't be uptight, don't faint,
        never doubt angels watch you and protect you.
    There's absolutely no doubt
        that angels encircle you
            and support you too.
Now don't bother to ask how.

Put that question out of your mind.
God says angels protect us;
therefore, it's certain.

ANGELS

This poor man called, and the Lord heard him,
He saved him out of all his troubles.
The angel of the Lord encamps around those who fear Him,
and He delivers them.
Taste and see that the Lord is good,
blessed is the man who takes refuge in Him.

Psalm 34:6-8

HIS PRESENCE

Ask God for Himself.
His presence is preeminent.

GOD'S WORD

In your own words, summarize the verses above.
What is the heart of this passage?
Do you know of someone who senses the care and comfort of angels?

SELF-EXAMINATION

What is the good news for you in these verses?
What sin, now uncovered, must you confess?
What will you do to strengthen your belief in God's care for you?

PETITION

Pray for yourself, in light of God's message.

INTERCESSION

Now you are ready to pray for others.

TEN

TEMPTATIONS AND TROUBLES

1. WHY CHRISTIANS LIVE ABOVE THREAT

Depression comes from the devil,
    especially the thought
        that God won't help us,
           that God won't be merciful.
    Whoever you are,
        burdened with these downers,
        know this without a doubt:
           Depression comes from Satan.
    God sent His Son
        not to frighten us
        but to comfort us.
So then, take courage.
You are not simply a human child,
    you are much more God's child through faith in Christ;
    you were baptized in His Name.
        Therefore, death can't stab you.

The devil has no right to you,
he can't hurt you,
he can't warp your thinking.

2. REAL SECURITY

Christian sorrow or worldly security—which is better?
It's better to be sorrowful,
to feel insecure from the world's perspective
and yet have the secure knowledge
of heaven because of Christ!
Remember what the psalmist wrote,
"God is pleased with those
who trust Him and His kindness."
Notice the two kinds of troubles:
Those that attack the spirit and
those that attack the body.
Satan attacks the spirit like this:
He tortures your conscience with lies,
he makes good biblical works look bad.
Never deliberately put a cross on your shoulders,
as some church people do.
But if a cross just comes to you,
shoulder it patiently,
knowing that it will profit you.

3. GOD AND OUR PROBLEMS

It's impossible
for human beings
without crosses and problems
to focus on God.

4. GREAT TROUBLES YIELD GREAT RESULTS

Clearly David suffered the attack of devils
      more than we;
otherwise he couldn't have had
      such revelations!
David created psalms
and we create them too.
      We sing to know the Lord God,
      and the devil and his spouse
      get their tails tied in knots.

5. HOLD ONTO GOD'S PROMISES

David sang sadly,
      "O Absalom, my son,
      my son, Absalom,
      my son."
            These words tell us
            that David suffered
            terrible grief and confusion.
Good King David had troubles!
Fear and horror grabbed him and
God's promises went dark on him.
But look what David did:
      He fastened his grip on God's sure Word.
            Now the value of that
            just cannot be calculated.

6. THE REAL ADVENTURE

The true Church's venture deals
      not only with flesh and blood
            but with evil power blocks at the top.

This is real adventure,
        like climbing a dangerous mountain.
Flesh and blood threaten you and me,
        our wives and children,
                houses, lands, furnishings—
                        but that's not the real adventure.
The real adventure?
        Overcoming spiritual evil
                that could rob us of soul,
                        heaven, and salvation.

7. THE GOD OF GENUINE HEARTS

Our God helps people who are
        humbled and puzzled,
        needy and troubled,
        afraid and endangered.
                If we had it made,
                we'd be proud and
                show off our stuff.
But God helps us when we're weak.
And He won't hit us when we're down.

8. FAITH'S TRIBULATION AND TRIUMPH

The most difficult torture
is faith's tribulation.
        Faith can rise above all problems.
        If faith gets frustrated,
                then we really have difficulties.
        But if faith is sound and well,
                she holds up her head,
                        she reduces vexations
                        and minimizes their effects!

An example of tribulation of faith
        is St. Paul's thorn
        which pierced body and spirit.
Another example is David, when he wrote,
    "Lord, don't reject me
    while You're angry."
    Surely David would have preferred
        death by the sword
        than to suffer the
        anger of God.

9. PSYCHOSOMATICS

Big burdens initiate physical hangups;
    an oppressed spirit means an oppressed body.
        Augustine saw this clearly.
Cares, thoughts that weigh you down,
    griefs, unchecked emotions,
        these rob us of energy and make us lifeless,
            like a horse minus get-up-and-go.
But when our hearts trust and find quiet,
    the body's needs are met.
The lesson: Let go of all anxieties.
    Indeed, resist them,
        and use any and all ways
            to do away with them.

10. DISCONTENT

Every human being knows discontent;
    no one knows trouble-free experience.
    Some have a need for troubles
    and create them!

No one lives just with the
    contentment God gives.

11. TO LIVE OR DIE

I sure would like to die now;
    I'm weak and strung out,
    yet I have joy,
            peace in my heart,
            a good conscience.
I know very well that
when health returns,
    I won't have peace or rest
    but I will have sorrow,
            fatigue, problems.
Even the great St. Paul
        did not escape challenges!

12. WE HAVE HELP

What do we say when spiritual troubles
head our way?
    "Why was I ever born?
    I'm sweating it out!"
But our Saviour, Christ,
suffered in the garden:
    "Father, please don't let Me
    drink this cup."
        His will confronted
        His Father's will,
        but He accepted God's will;
            then came the angel's comfort.
Jesus, in a body like ours,
faced plague and temptation.

Just there lies the reason
He is such a good go-between
and advocate for you and me
in our hard times:
>He becomes President
>when we let Him mediate,
>>when we are content
>>just to respond to His help.
When we go through trials and temptations,
it seems for all the world
that God dislikes us.
>When we repent of those feelings
>and believe Him once more,
>>we make a great discovery:
>>God's supposed anger is grace,
>>but grace has a way of hiding.
So let's patiently wait
God's time for release,
and always stay hopeful.

13. PERSPECTIVE

On August 8, 1529,
my Katie confined herself to bed
>with a fever,
>agonizing sciatica,
>and a dozen other physical problems.
>>God's been rough on me!
>>I've been impatient!
>>>Yet God knows better than I
>>>the purpose in all this.
God is like a printer
who sets the letters backwards
so we have difficulty reading.

But when God shows us the printout in heaven,
reading will come clear and easy.
Until then, don't panic.
The school called Trouble teaches us well.
Almost every verse of the psalms
   refers to troubles, puzzlements, sadness,
      tough and rough experiences.
         Psalms
         is a book
         of tribulations.

14. DON'T WORRY, BUT DON'T TAKE MERCY FOR GRANTED EITHER

Christ forgave the thief on the cross.
Christ forgave Paul,
   after blasphemy and persecution.
So we needn't doubt His mercy for us.
      Indeed, all of us
      come to salvation
      by His graciousness.
Though we have no reason
to fear God's wrath,
we'd better respect Him!
Adam did.
   We don't have capacity to grasp
   as firmly as we ought
   God's mercy and grace.
      Adam knew only the first part
      of the Creed:
         "I believe in God the Father."
         Yet, this knowledge went way
         beyond his natural wisdom,
         reason, and comprehension.

15. HOW TO DEFEND YOURSELF

Just as rain usually falls
    where it's already wet,
        so the devil attacks me
            at my most vulnerable spot.
When doubt possesses you,
    God seems to turn a deaf ear,
    God seems to turn Himself away,
    God seems to be angry.
        Your thoughts disturb you;
        they seem forced on you.
            Just then arm yourself with God's Word;
never mind when or where or how
    God will hear you. Just know He will.
    God's promise—
    Ah! That's sure and substantial.

16. I NEED SOMEONE TO TALK TO

When I'm troubled
I often need to talk to someone,
    even a child,
    to get rid of the thoughts
    the devil corners me with.
This catharsis teaches me
    not to boast.
        I can't go it alone and
        I can't exist aside from
        Christ's strength.
I need people.
        At times I need help,
        even from someone who
        is theologically ignorant.

17. DEGREES OF SUFFERING

People suffer at different levels.
Someone could have suffered my afflictions
only to die by this time.
I could not face St. Paul's attacks,
nor could St. Paul face Christ's sufferings.
The biggest grief comes when
a loved one dies suddenly.
But don't allow yourself a hangup;
just let God handle it.

18. KEEPING PIGS

When I am weary with problems,
I go tend my pigs;
I do not let myself
go round and round,
pondering my troubles.
The human heart
is like
a millstone
in a flour mill:
When it grinds wheat
it produces flour;
when it grinds without wheat,
it wears itself down.
The human heart's just like that:
unless it's occupied with employment,
the devil works into the empty space
with bad thoughts,
temptations,
and hangups
which wear us down.

19. I NEED CHALLENGES MORE THAN BREAD

You who experience problems—
get used to them.
Learn to hang in there!
    You need challenges more than
    you need meat and bread.
    If Satan hadn't given me a bad time,
        I never would have exercised the faith muscle
            to develop it to fight with effectiveness.
More, threat keeps us from pride,
    thus increasing our acknowledgment
        of Christ, God's gifts and blessings.
From my first tribulations,
    God gave me victory
    to overcome what's really evil.
        God did the business in such a way
        that no government ruler
        or church authority
            could stop my work.
When the devil gave me a bad time,
    God made everybody aware of
        His strength in my weakness.

20. SAY A FIRM "NO!"

When the devil plagues you
with troubles and doubts,
drive him away successfully
with a decided, "Get lost!"
    When you meet an angry dog,
    if you keep your cool and talk firmly,
        the cur won't bite you,
        he even stops barking.

But if you show fear,
or throw something at him,
he lunges at you and
may bite you too.
Just so, when the devil senses you're afraid,
he jumps all over you.

21. SPIRITUAL HEALING

Case history: The very sick woman of Eisenach,
who had unbelievable attacks
that no doctor could cure.
Clearly the devil did the dirty work.
She went into faints;
she had some sort of fits.
These faintings and fits
lasted three or four hours.
Her hands and feet assumed
a horn shape, quite bent.
She took chills. Her body swelled.
Her tongue turned rough and dry.
When I went to visit her,
she delighted in seeing me,
sat up, and said,
"My loving spiritual father,
I carry a great weight;
pray for me."
Then she lay down again.
With this, I put Satan in his place,
and commanded peace for this child of God.
I turned to those nearby to say,
"She's suffering a bodily attack by the devil,
but her soul is okay and God will preserve her;
so let's praise Him and pray for her."

Then they all prayed the Lord's Prayer out loud.
>Next, I prayed,
>>"Our Heavenly Father,
>>our Lord God,
>>>You assigned us to pray for sick people,
>>>so we ask You through Jesus Christ,
>>>the only and beloved Son,
>>>to deliver her from illness and Satan.
>>>Keep her soul and body which You bought
>>>from sin's power and the devil."
>With this, the woman said, "Amen."
>>That night she slept and
>>the next day she was totally well,
>>>fully delivered.

22. HANG IN THERE PATIENTLY

When Satan tempts you nonstop,
>hang in there anyway.
Hold on with both hands and both feet;
don't faint as if there were no end in view;
>stand courageously and wait
>patiently for God's time of release.
But heighten your awareness.
>>What Satan cannot achieve
>>>by sudden impact,
>>he will try to do by subtlety
>>>and vexation that seems endless.
This is what the psalmist refers to:
>>"Since my youth,
>>frequent temptations come,
>>but they've never succeeded."
In all this, note your assured security:
>God always wins against the devil.

Moreover, the angels help you win.
   And God, with the angels,
   gets great pleasure out of your
   spiritual victory.
      So, assure yourself
      that at the end of the road
      is happiness!
      At the close of the fight,
      eternal comfort!

23. REFUSE TO WORRY ABOUT PREDESTINATION

On predestination,
  start with Christ
in whom we find the Father.
    If you start by trying to
    sort out God's will,
    you could break your neck!
I've gone through torture on this issue.
    I wanted to know if God elected me!
Praise God, I stopped the inner debate when
I took a good grip on God's revealed Word.
    Beyond this I could settle nothing,
    for finite thinkers cannot figure out
      the Celestial Thinker.
    God hides His explanation
    so the crafty will be deceived,
      and will be confused.
    God reveals some things
      and hides other things.
The last word and all we need:
  Know Christ who is like us, and
    the Father revealed in Him.

24. CHRIST'S PROBLEMS

One day Jesus came into Jerusalem;
A few days later He died on a cross.
    He carried a big burden about sin,
    about God's anger, about death
    —all could have frightened Him.
        He took our sins on Himself;
        He took our sorrows and our griefs.
        He felt very hurt because
His own people said no
to His offer of salvation;
        He wept a great deal,
        and experienced bitterness too,
        because they let their
        opportunity go by.

25. SIN AND PRIVACY

Most sins,
    and the biggest sins,
    are committed in private.
        Fewer sins happen in groups.
        Eve walked alone
        and the devil deceived her.
In hidden places people murder,
    rob, and commit adultery.
The reason?
    The devil takes advantage of solitude
    to misdirect people.
    In a group of good people, however,
        shame may stop sin.
    Also, the opportunity to do something wrong
        is not so great.

Remember Jesus' promise:
    "Where two or three
    come together in My Name,
    I'm with them."
Idle and alone,
    David went AWOL,
    committed adultery
    and murder.
I discovered this about myself:
Most of my sins I do alone.
God created us for fellowship,
Not aloneness.

26. WHEN CHRIST NEEDED HUMAN SUPPORT

Christ suffered more than anyone in history.
    His sorrow produced sweat and blood.
       No one can understand this,
          but the result was wonderful.
Yet it seems almost more wonderful that
    the Lord of grace and wrath,
       the Lord of life and death,
          should be really human.
    He was weak and sad.
       He sought comfort from ordinary sinners:
          "Dear disciples, don't go to sleep;
          stay awake with Me;
          talk so I can hear someone near Me."
    Remember the Psalm that says,
       "God made him a little
       lower than the angels."
His bloody sweat reflected
an immeasurable burden.

Our beautiful Saviour suffered that!
He carried the sins of the whole world!
    No doubt He prayed like this:
        "O Lord,
        don't reject Me in
        Your anger;
        don't chasten Me in
        the heat of Your displeasure."

TEMPTATIONS AND TROUBLES

He too shared in their humanity so that by His death He might destroy him who holds the power of death—that is, the devil—and free those who all their lives were held in slavery by their fear of death. . . . For this reason He had to be made like His brothers in every way, in order that He might become a merciful and faithful high priest in service to God, and that He might make atonement for the sins of the people. Because He Himself suffered when He was tempted, He is able to help those who are being tempted.   Hebrews 2:14-18

HIS PRESENCE

Ask God for Himself.
His presence is preeminent.

GOD'S WORD

Can you think of other Scriptures on temptation?

SELF-EXAMINATION

What will you do to enhance your faith in Christ's work for you?

PETITION

Pray for yourself, in light of God's message.

INTERCESSION

Now you are ready to pray for others.

ELEVEN

HEALTH AND HEALING

1. BABIES CRY AND DEVELOP

It is good that babies cry heartily.
    They grow well and
    they grow fast,
        because crying stretches them
        and gives them exercise
        they wouldn't have otherwise.

2. DOES SIN CAUSE ILLNESS?

Jesus said to the man sick with shaking,
        "Cheer up, son;
        I forgive your sins."
            Christ seems to suggest
            sin caused the palsy.
But in John we read about
the man born blind:

"His parents didn't sin;
the man didn't sin."
The message:
Sin didn't cause the blindness.
Active sins done personally
cause illnesses and epidemics.
But original sin
doesn't produce them.
So the shaking man sinned
and got palsy;
The blind man suffered original sin,
but that didn't cause his sightlessness;
otherwise, everyone would be born blind.

3. SLEEP

Want help?
Sleep helps.
Sleep heals.
Of the minor annoyances,
sudden awakening from
a peaceful slumber
angers me most.
In Italy, I'm told,
poor people are tortured
by depriving them of sleep.
Such torture cannot be long endured.

4. HIGHER AND LOWER MEDICINE

Doctors look for natural causes;
sometimes they cure illness,
sometimes they don't.

They may not detect
the work of the devil.
A higher medicine
routs the devil's maladies.
What is this higher medicine?
Faith and prayer.
What is the source of higher medicine?
God's Word, as in Psalm 31,
where David says,
"Into Your hand
I commit
my spirit."
This passage I learned
in my illness.
At first I thought Psalm 31
related only to death.
Now I see its larger meaning:
"Into Your hand
I commit
my health and happiness,
my misfortune and illness,
my very life."
You see,
every aspect of wholeness
rests in God's hands.
We say,
"Get joyful. Get merry.
Be relaxed. Be healthy."
But we may end up
just the opposite!
When I was ill at Schmalcalden,
my doctors gave me
enough medicine
to treat a large bull!

Woe to him who depends
only on medicine.
Sure, medicine is God's gift,
but I know no perfect doctor,
not even the best is perfect.
Sound procedures produce sound results.
When I feel ill,
careful diet and
a good night's sleep
generally do the job,
provided I keep my mind
at reasonable rest.
Let the doctors have their theories,
but we're not slaves to them!
Physicians in other centuries
tried different treatments.
I don't put uncritical faith in
any remedy, ancient or modern.
Watch out for ignorant doctors.
These characters,
unbending in their therapies,
send patients to their graves!
Capable, careful, seasoned doctors—
these are God's gifts.
Yet, a moment's carelessness can
put a sick person in a bind.
Physicians must do all their work
in humility and in respect for God.
Swaggering doctors are criminals.
Exercise and fresh air help,
sometimes more than treatment,
but when we take medicine,
we must follow the directions
of judicious doctors.

Note what happened to Peter Lupinus:
    He took external medication
    internally, and he died.
Then there was another case,
this one involving a lawsuit:
    It arose over the administration
    of apium instead of opium.

5. AUTHORITY AND THERAPY

Princes and lords apply some remedies
successfully,
sometimes when physicians are
unsuccessful.
    John and Frederic,
    electors of Saxony,
    have a water that
    cures eye diseases
        . . . when *they* use it.
    It doesn't work when
    physicians administer it.
So in spiritual things:
    A preacher exercises more power
    and sees better results
    on moral cures than a layperson.

HEALTH AND HEALING

Now a man crippled from birth was being carried to the temple gate called Beautiful, where he was put every day to beg from those going into the temple courts. When he saw Peter and John about to enter, he asked them for money. Then Peter said, "Silver or gold I do not have, but what I have I give you. In the name of Jesus Christ of Nazareth, walk." Taking him by the right hand, he helped him up, and instantly the man's feet and ankles became strong. He . . . went with them into the temple courts, walking and jumping, and praising God.

Acts 3:2-3, 6-8

HIS PRESENCE

Ask God for Himself.
His presence is preeminent.

GOD'S WORD

What is the heart of this passage?

SELF-EXAMINATION

What is the good news for you in these verses?

PETITION

Pray for yourself, in light of God's message.

INTERCESSION

Now you are ready to pray for others.

TWELVE

RESURRECTION

1. LUTHER'S EASTER SERMON, 1544

Text:
 "Come alive to this truth—
 What you sow
 comes up
 only after it dies."
Case Study: Abraham.
 Abraham believed that from
 the sacrifice of his son,
  God would bring Isaac to life and
  through him create a race of people.
Believers know anything is possible.
 Take conception and birth.
 From a mere drop of blood,
  so to speak,
comes a miracle,
the wonder work of God.

Adam came from dirt,
Eve from a rib.
    The world's full of
    such wonders,
    but we're blind to them.
Look at these resurrection words:
  "Get up.
Come.
Stand.
Appear.
Be happy,
    you who live
    in this earthly world."
God will make a new heaven
and a new earth,
where only good lives.
    No desert,
    only beauty.
No carnivorous beasts,
no poisonous animals,
no sin in anybody or anything.
Just friendliness as in Eden,
and little yellow dogs
shining like gems.
Trees in full foliage,
grass green as emeralds.
    And how about us?
    No bad appetites.
    No compulsions.
    Good desires in full flower.
    Godly perspective.
    No sickness.
    No tribulations.
    God—we'll see Him.

Loved ones and friends:
Perfect harmony and
perfect peace with them.
Why not all this good now?
Our hangups here
make us yearn for a
trouble-free life there.
But if God's own have joy there,
the unsaved will know
the worst sorrow
and terrible despair.

2. LUTHER'S AUGUST 7, 1538 TALK ABOUT HEAVEN

Recently ill and very weak,
I told God again that
He could do anything
He wished with me.
In bed I reflected a lot
about everlasting life:
We'll have joy.
We'll know the full meaning
of what Christ said,
it's already ours
and we believe it,
but it will come clear,
full circle.
We can't know here
the nature of the next life,
because this temporal world
hides the eternal world.
Here we work with the
visible and physical.

Everlasting joys go
beyond human comprehension.
Isaiah exclaimed:
    "You will know
    eternal joy,
    glorious joy!"
Why don't we believe Scripture?
    Eternal life is sure!
    The Resurrection is coming fact!
        Original sin blinds us to all this.
    The unsaved will see what they're missing,
        thus enhancing their torture.
God made our wonderful passing world,
    its sky,
    its earth,
    its delights.
        But the next world—
        more delightful!
        More glorious!
            His kingdom
            nonstop for eternity!

3. OUTSIDE OUR PRESENT EXPERIENCE

As a baby taking
mother's milk,
    I could not know
    about eating a beautiful meal
    at a nicely set table.
Just so,
    living here on earth
    I cannot comprehend
    the life to come.

4. HELL

With all my heart I want
Zuinglius saved,
but how can he be?
    Christ said those who
    deny Him
    go to hell.
        God's judgment is
        sure and certain,
        we know it will
        come to the ungodly.
With all his heart David wanted
Absalom saved.
    "Absalom my son,
    Absalom my son,"
    David cried,
        yet he believed his son lost,
        mourned him because
        he died and was lost,
            he died in rebellion,
            in incest,
            in hunting his father
            out of his kingdom.

5. COME QUICKLY

O loving God,
don't put off coming,
    I wait impatiently
    for the return of spring,
        when day and night are of equal length,
        when the Aurora is clear and bright in the sky.
One day we'll see a black cloud,

flashes of lightning,
a clap of thunder,
confusion covering earth and sky.
        Then! we will praise the Lord
        who taught us to want
        that Day very much.
        I hope the Day comes soon.
Some fear that Day.
        Jesus said,
        "On that Day,
        faith
        will be hard to find."
Take a good look.
Faith lives only in a corner,
        not in Asia and Africa,
        nor in Europe.
                This little corner, Saxony,
                won't hinder the coming of
                the Last Judgment Day.
Many Bible predictions
        have already come true;
        the world can't last much longer;
                Scripture will come true.
Christ will come:
        "The Lord of all says that,
        in a little while
        He will shake the heavens,
        the earth, the nations;
        the dream of all nations
                will come true."
At the end expect great changes
and lots of commotion.
        Already we see commotion:
                Law enforcement people stay busy;

families break up;
the Church suffers disharmony.

RESURRECTION

On His arrival, Jesus found that Lazarus had already
been in the tomb for four days. . . . "Lord," Martha
said to Jesus, "if You had been here, my brother
would not have died."

Jesus said to her, "I am the resurrection and the
life. . . . whoever lives and believes in Me will never
die. Do you believe this?"

"Yes, Lord," she told Him, "I believe that You are
the Christ, the Son of God, who was to come into
the world."   John 11:17, 21, 25-27

HIS PRESENCE

Ask God for Himself.
His presence is preeminent.

GOD'S WORD

What is the heart of this passage?
Do you live with unquestioned belief in the hope of heaven?

SELF-EXAMINATION

What will you do to live with an eye to eternity?

PETITION

Pray for yourself, in light of God's message.

INTERCESSION

Now you are ready to pray for others.

MARTIN LUTHER BIBLIOGRAPHY

These books may help you understand Martin Luther's life and thought.

Bainton, Roland H. *Here I Stand: A Life of Martin Luther*. Nashville: Abingdon, 1950.

Bell, Captain Henry, translator. *From the Table Talk of Martin Luther*. London and New York: Cassell and Company, Ltd., 1886.

Doberstein, John W., editor. *A Lutheran Prayer Book*. Philadelphia: Fortress Press, 1967.

————, editor. *Minister's Prayer Book: An Order of Prayers and Readings*. Philadelphia: Fortress Press, 1986 (reprint). (Doberstein's introduction included.)

Eerdman's Handbook to the History of Christianity. Grand Rapids: Eerdmans, 1977.

Hilderbrand, Hans J. *The Reformation: A Narrative History Related by Contemporary Observers and Participants*. New York: Harper and Row, 1964.

Jones, Cheslyn, Geoffrey Wainwright, and Edward Yarnold, editors. *The Study of Spirituality*. New York: Oxford, 1986.

Kepler, Thomas S., editor. *The Table Talk of Martin Luther*. Grand Rapids: Baker Book House, 1952. (Kepler's introduction included.)

Tappert, Theodore G., editor and translator, *Luther's Works*, Vol. 54: *Table Talk*. Philadelphia: Fortress Press, 1967.

Zundel, Veronica, compiler. *Eerdman's Book of Christian Classics: A Treasury of Christian Writings through the Centuries*. Grand Rapids: Eerdmans, 1985.

FOR FURTHER READING

The following materials are suggested to help you increase your understanding of Spiritual Formation, and more importantly, to help you grow in your faith. Readings are categorized under basic headings having to do with our formation. Most of the books are in print at the time of this compilation. The few which are not can be obtained from most college and seminary libraries in your area.

General Readings

1. Leslie Weatherhead, *The Transforming Friendship*
2. Steve Harper, *Devotional Life in the Wesleyan Tradition*
3. Maxie Dunnam, *Alive in Christ*
4. E. Stanley Jones, *The Way*
5. Henri Nouwen, *Making All Things New*
6. Evelyn Underhill, *The Spiritual Life*
7. Alan Jones and Rachel Hosmer, *Living in the Spirit*
8. Iris Cully, *Education for Spiritual Growth*
9. Benedict Groeschel, *Spiritual Passages*

Scripture

1. Robert Mulholland, *Shaped by the Word*
2. David Thompson, *Bible Study That Works*
3. Susan Muto, *A Practical Guide to Spiritual Reading*
4. Thomas Merton, *Opening the Bible*
5. H. A. Nielsen, *The Bible as if for the First Time*
6. Robert Traina, *Methodical Bible Study*

Prayer
1. Harry E. Fosdick, *The Meaning of Prayer*
2. Dick Eastman, *The Hour That Changes the World*
3. Kenneth Leech, *True Prayer*
4. Anthony Bloom, *Beginning to Pray*
5. Maxie Dunnam, *The Workbook of Living Prayer*
6. O. Hallesby, *Prayer*

The Lord's Supper
1. William Willimon, *Sunday Dinner*
2. William Barclay, *The Lord's Supper*
3. Martin Marty, *The Lord's Supper*

Fasting
1. Richard Foster, *Celebration of Discipline* (helpful chapter)
2. Tilden Edwards, *Living Simply through the Day* (helpful chapter)

Direction/Accountability
1. David Watson, *Accountable Discipleship*
2. Tilden Edwards, *Spiritual Friend*
3. Kenneth Leech, *Soul Friend*
4. Robert Coleman, *The Master Plan of Evangelism*

Personality and Spiritual Development
1. David Keirsey, *Please Understand Me*
2. Harold Grant, *From Image to Likeness*
3. Christopher Bryant, *The River Within*
4. Chester Michael, *Prayer and Temperament*

The Holy Spirit
1. Billy Graham, *The Holy Spirit*
2. Kenneth Kinghorn, *The Gifts of the Spirit*

3. Myron Augsburger, *Quench Not the Spirit*

Discipline and Disciplines
1. Richard Foster, *Celebration of Discipline*
2. Gordon MacDonald, *Ordering Your Private World*
3. Albert E. Day, *Discipline and Discovery*
4. James Earl Massey, *Spiritual Disciplines*
5. Maxie Dunnam, *The Workbook of Spiritual Disciplines*

History of Christian Spirituality
1. Urban Holmes, *A History of Christian Spirituality*
2. Alan Jones and Rachel Hosmer, *Living in the Spirit* (helpful chapter)

Devotional Classics (Introduction to)
1. Thomas à Kempis, *Imitation of Christ*
2. Tilden Edwards, *The Living Testament: The Essential Writings since the New Testament*
3. Thomas Kepler, *An Anthology of Devotional Literature*
4. Brother Lawrence, *Practice of the Presence of God*
5. *The Upper Room Devotional Classics*
6. Paulist Press Series, *The Classics of Western Spirituality*

Social Spirituality
1. John Carmody, *Holistic Spirituality*
2. John Carmody, *Maturing a Christian Conscience*
3. William Stringfellow, *The Politics of Spirituality*
4. Dietrich Bonhoeffer, *Life Together*
5. Thomas Kelly, *A Testament of Devotion* (helpful chapter)
6. Henri Nouwen, *Gracias!*
7. Henri Nouwen, *Compassion*

Ministry and Spiritual Formation

1. Edward Bratcher, *The Walk-on-Water Syndrome*
2. Henri Nouwen, *The Living Reminder*
3. Louis McBirney, *Every Pastor Needs a Pastor*
4. Henri Nouwen, *Creative Ministry*
5. Oswald Sanders, *Spiritual Leadership*

Devotional Guides and Prayer Books

1. Rueben Job, *The Upper Room Guide to Prayer for Ministers and Other Servants*
2. Bob Benson, *Disciplines for the Inner Life*
3. John Baille, *A Diary of Private Prayer*
4. Charles Swindoll, *Growing Strong in the Seasons of Life*
5. John Doberstein, *The Minister's Prayer Book*
6. *The Book of Common Prayer*